Digital

Reduce Costs and Improve Efficiency using Robotic Process Automation

RPA

Rob King

Digital Workforce

Reduce Costs and Improve Efficiency using Robotic Process Automation

Rob King

Rob King has asserted his moral right to be identified as the author of this work in accordance with the Copyright, Design and Patents Act 1988.

All rights reserved. No part of this publication may be reproduced, stored in a retrieval system, or transmitted in any form or by any means, electronic, mechanical, photocopying, recording or otherwise, without the prior written consent of the copyright owner.

Disclaimer

The Author shall have neither liability nor responsibility to any person or entity with respect to any loss or damage caused, or alleged to have been caused, directly or indirectly, by the information contained in this book.

© 2018 Rob King

For Mum and Dad

Contents

Introduction i

Acknowledgements vii

Understanding RPA 1

1. What is Robotic Process Automation? 3
   A View of the RPA Market 4
   Defining Robotic Process Automation 8

2. Why Might I Need A Digital Workforce? 29
   Considerations before You Automate 30
   Reasons to Automate Now 33
   Delivering your Business Case 37
   Examples of Automation 43

Getting Started 49

3. Taking a Business-First Approach 51
   Assessing Your Business Needs 53
   Developing Your Strategy 64
   Setting Expectations 69

4. The Automation Vendors 79
   Selecting your Automation Technology 83

CONTENTS

    Assessing Vendor Capabilities 84
    Assessing the RPA Vendors 90
    Example Scenarios for Shortlisting Vendors 108

5. Getting Started with a Pilot **115**
    Stakeholders and Vocabulary 117
    Where to Begin 120
    Building your Team .121
    Selecting your first Process 127
    Advantages of a Pilot Study 129
    Measurement: Critical Success Factors 133
    Running and Evaluating a Pilot 142

Scaling Up 145

6. Six Key Responsibilities **147**
    1. Senior Leader 150
    2. Business Process Improver 152
    3. Business Architect 156
    4. Technical (or Enterprise) Architect 158
    5. RPA Developer 161
    6. Operations Support 165

7. Applying Lean Thinking to RPA **167**
    Getting Started with Lean RPA 169
    Scaling Up with Lean RPA 171
    Customer Demand: Runners, Repeaters, Rogues . .174
    Optimising Processes using Lean Thinking 180

8. Prioritising Processes for Continuous Delivery . . .**183**
    The Process Prioritisation Funnel 184
    Process Prioritisation Criteria 192
    Continuous Delivery 198

Transformation 201

9. Developing a Target Operating Model .... .203
    Maturity Model .... .205
    Operating Model .... .210
    The Role of IT .... .216
    Fine Tuning CoE Responsibilities .... .222

10. Digital Workforce Evolution .... .231
    The Automation Delivery Lifecycle (ADLC) ..... .232
    RPA Automation Model .... .234
    Intelligent Automation Model .... .236
    Digital Transformation and Innovation .... .238
    The Next Phase for Automation .... .240
    Conclusion .... .244

Appendix 247

Questions Answered .... .249

Glossary .... .261

Introduction

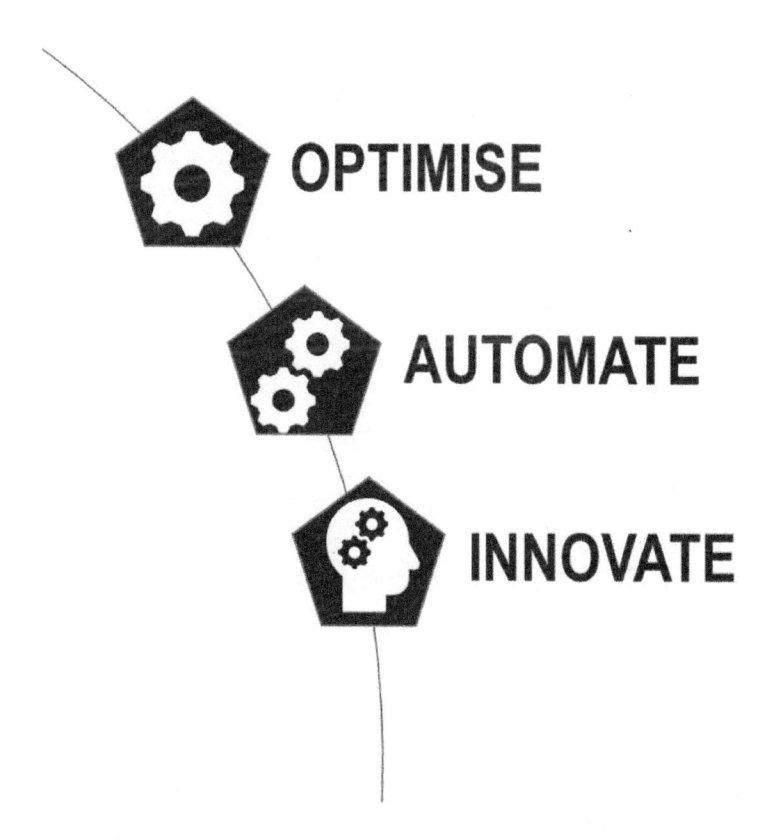

OPTIMISE

AUTOMATE

INNOVATE

Since 2012 I've found myself increasingly immersed in the topic of Robotic Process Automation (RPA). I first discovered the existence of RPA when leading a lean transformation programme and found that it provided new opportunities to improve efficiency, reduce costs and prevent errors. Since then my involvement has steadily grown to where it is today: speaking at conferences, blogging and consulting with organisations interested in learning more about the opportunity for introducing RPA to create their own digital workforce.

> A Digital Workforce.

Perhaps surprisingly, RPA has more similarities with your human workforce than with the typical software licenced to run on your desktop. When considering automation you can now implement full-time robots, part-time robots and even bring on board some temporary robots to meet a short-term peak in demand. In other words, a Digital Workforce requires the same management and planning that you currently use to deliver your current business outcomes.

It's more than a mirror of your existing human workforce though; it's a workforce capable of operating 24/7, delivering output to a high quality and carrying out the most mundane and repetitive tasks to the same standard every time. It needs managing, governing, performance monitoring and, when regulation changes, retraining - just like your human workforce.

It may have seemed that RPA was something only for the large corporations, as early adopters were global institutions, banks and financial services. It was the case that if you couldn't afford one of the big accounting and consulting firms to implement it for you, then don't bother. But that's simply not true anymore and the purpose of this book is to help demonstrate that RPA is an opportunity for any business of any size.

> A Digital Workforce can benefit any organisation, however big or small.

Over the last 5 years the market has changed dramatically; costs, capabilities and opportunities have accelerated at an unprecedented pace and the solutions are immensely capable and provide options for everyone.

But what is holding people back? Misunderstandings? Too technical? It isn't for me? It's stealing my job? I could fill this introduction with all the reasons that I've heard *not* to start. But the truth is, the barriers to entry have been falling, a Digital Workforce is *not* outside the reach of anyone and everyone can benefit.

> A Digital Workforce can increase efficiency, quality, customer satisfaction, and reduce costs.

In preparing this book I've talked to hundreds of industry insiders, vendors and early adopters to understand their challenges and opportunities. I first implemented RPA successfully, then unsuccessfully, in 2013. The challenges that set us back the most were rarely technical – although there were certainly a few of those along the way – but rather cultural and behavioural obstacles.

The introduction of new technologies and innovation has been a focus throughout my career and one consistent nugget of wisdom that I've taken away from numerous projects is that the technology (when selected correctly) broadly works. It's the organisational culture, fear of change, and poor adoption that prevents the full benefits from being realised. The same is true for RPA.

> A Digital Workforce introduces new innovative opportunities and a few cultural challenges!

It's an exciting time; the sheer variety of options available, the direction of travel as a gateway to introducing Artificial

Intelligence (AI) and working with businesses exploring RPA for the first time are all providing new opportunities to expand your business. It has always been a personal ambition to write a book one day and I've been aware that when you search for a book on RPA there are very few independent choices available.

It all seemed the right time to bring together the information I've accumulated over the past 18 months of consulting, public speaking and blogging into a single place, the book you're holding. When anyone asked questions in a typical conference or speaking engagement, there was never the time to give what I would say was a sufficiently complete response. The questions that come up all the time are:

- Where do I begin?
- Which is the best solution?
- How do I find the right process?
- How do I develop a business case?

The phrasing of these questions implies that there's a simple answer. Unfortunately, that is simply not the case; RPA doesn't provide the silver bullet to answer them with a simple single truth. However, RPA *is* the technology that will allow you to develop a Digital Workforce and solve real business problems that you're facing today.

> A Digital Workforce is a solution to address common business problems.

My goals in writing this book are to introduce RPA to businesses who thought it out of their reach; to provide a roadmap for implementing RPA; and to deliver more thoughtful responses to the common questions that I never have the time to answer in brief conference discussions.

This isn't a technical book. As the manuscript developed from concept to words on a page, it became clear that this was about the process, the people and the cultural challenges that you'll face. Digital Workforce is a title that encapsulates what this book is about as RPA will only be successful when the technology is combined with the right processes and the right culture.

It starts with you: a Digital Workforce is the solution to many of the problems and opportunities you'll be facing in your industry today.

This book is divided into four sections:

Section one: Understanding Robotic Process Automation explains what RPA is and why it might be something that you need.

Section two: Getting Started with a Digital Workforce helps you identify your business needs to narrow down to a list of suitable products capable of meeting your requirements and embark on your first automation project: preparing, delivering and monitoring your first robot.

Section three: Scaling Up your Digital Workforce looks at the roles and responsibilities needed, introduces you to a few helpful lean thinking techniques and establishes a process prioritisation funnel to begin feeding your engine room of development.

Section four: Transforming your Digital Workforce focuses on operating models to understand the different approaches available, including the most common, a dedicated function known as a Centre of Excellence (CoE). It looks at the Automation Delivery Lifecycle; the steps to sustaining your automation programme. Finally, you'll see how RPA provides a useful stepping-stone to introducing innovative ideas and AI-led solutions.

At the end of each chapter you'll find a series of optional exercises. Collectively these exercises operate like a workbook, helping you to structure your thoughts on your own RPA programme.

Developing a *digital workforce* is an opportunity for every business with options to fit every need. This book will help you to begin your automation journey. Thank you for reading.

Rob King
September 2018

Acknowledgements

I'd like to thank my business partner Rod Willmott for first introducing me to the topic of RPA and continuing to encourage me through the year long journey of bringing this book to life.

I'd especially like to thank Liz James at Purple Prose Solutions[1] who went above and beyond the call of duty while proofreading, editing and enhancing the materials, helping to clarify the topics I was trying to explain.

To my teams at LV= who shared the blood, sweat and tears that go alongside implementing RPA.

Along my RPA journey, I've met many new people who have become friends and colleagues, but a special mention is due to Martin Macnair and Leigh Varnham; they were there at the very start, working on the vendor side, and have since become good friends. This book would never have happened if we hadn't met.

To my test subjects, who kindly endured early copies of the manuscript and helped provide clarity and structure to the book you hold today.

Last, but not least, to my family: my wife, Dee, and sons, Callum and Blake, who have all been my inspiration to keep going. Even when I realised that the Pareto principle was becoming painfully true and the last 20% really did require 80% of the effort!

---

[1] https://www.linkedin.com/in/liz-james-winchester/

Understanding RPA

1. What is Robotic Process Automation?

A View of the RPA Market

I've been fortunate enough to see many of the industry changes first-hand as the potential for RPA has been recognised. RPA has moved from relative obscurity and matured into a reliable, sustainable business solution capable of delivering new business value.

When I began looking at RPA in 2012, few of the current market leaders had any presence. While most of today's leading vendors existed, the technology was still developing and new entrants with sufficient funding and vision were looking to develop their market share. Even though new companies are still joining the market today, I believe that the current leaders are unlikely to change at this stage. The market opportunity is huge, so there are still significant business opportunities for existing suppliers.

Globally the RPA market was estimated at $271 million in 2016, increased to $443 million in 2017 and is expected to grow to $1.2 billion by 2021[2]. When you include into these numbers the impact of introducing RPA in combination with AI, the predictions increase to $15.4 billion by 2021[3]. RPA is a significant area of business focus and adding AI into the mix ensures it will continue to be so for many years to come.

The impact of RPA is expected to be so significant that it is already being considered as a key driver in the Fourth Industrial Revolution. The advances in digital technology have the potential to change the nature of work radically, introducing a new *Digital Workforce* that operates alongside

---

[2] Horses for Sources Analysis https://www.horsesforsources.com/RPA-marketsize-HfS_061017

[3] Horses for Sources Analysis https://www.horsesforsources.com/automation-AI%20forecast_110417

the existing human one. Society, culture and economics are all being impacted by the disruption that RPA technologies can introduce. Industry commentators have been quick to call out prophecies of doom with job losses in the millions, while others predict a rebalancing effect offering new roles and new challenges to be explored. There is absolutely no doubt that RPA means there will be radical changes in the way we currently work.

Businesses will *have* to adopt new operating models to survive; automation is the enabler. People will be displaced but new jobs requiring new skills will be created. And, as automation increasingly includes elements of learning and intelligence, it'll be essential for regulated industries to demonstrate their compliance, increasing their immediate need for data science skills.

Financial services, and particularly the banks, are now very much driven by the need to cut costs, increase quality and address changing customer demands. The sector has been quick to embrace RPA, as it meets all these needs perfectly. Despite this, they have only implemented a small percentage of possible processes so far and many other industry sectors have barely begun[4].

Business Process Outsourcing (BPO) is already one of the most significantly disrupted industries. This is an industry where simple and repetitive tasks have been moved off-shore where labour costs are cheaper. These are exactly the types of processes that can easily be completed by RPA. Some outsourcers have been quick to identify the need for change and have been adopting RPA as a way to continue running the outsourced operations. Even so, the

---

[4] Everest Group 2018 identified 38% of the total RPA Market Share as Financial Services. https://www2.everestgrp.com/reportaction/EGR-2018-38-R-2691/Marketing

economics of outsourcing an offshore *digital workforce* will leave questions as to whether it is now more cost effective to bring the business back onshore, eliminating the need for offshore operations entirely.

The number of RPA tools is growing consistently but it's difficult to imagine that new entrants will be capable of achieving enough market share and be anything other than niche players, some will simply not survive. The market-leading vendors have all made significant partnership arrangements to defend their position or have obtained large funding deals to grow their market share. In this climate, new entrants and smaller suppliers will find it difficult to compete.

Resource Shortage[5]

Concerns about the shortage of RPA resources are a constant topic of conversation in the industry and this is a challenge for all organisations. On the positive side, a wide variety of vendor-led and third-party training options have been developed to accelerate growth and meet the increased demand. The skills pool is diluted by the sheer number of RPA technologies which spread the already limited resources across multiple products. The problem will diminish as the market leaders with a stronger track record of delivery attract a greater percentage of new customers.

As the shortage of technical skills is slowly being addressed, another problem is emerging. The skills to manage and implement new operating models and sustain the change are equally scarce and in greater demand. Hybrid

---

[5] Everest Group 2018 identified resource shortage as the Number 1 inhibitor to RPA growth. https://www2.everestgrp.com/reportaction/EGR-2018-38-R-2691/Marketing

skills, involving both business *and* technology, will be very much in demand and, at the same time, automation skills will increasingly be found in technology savvy business people.

Challenging Cultural Change

The most complex and difficult thing to change will be the culture of your business. People rarely like change, and even the most open-minded will take time to work through the emotions associated with any change of significance. We can already learn lessons from companies that have managed this well: thinking of their people first and putting clear and thoughtful communication at the forefront of their agenda. Defeat can easily be snatched from the jaws of victory if not enough thought and time is given to people and culture.

Defining Robotic Process Automation

The first step in understanding RPA is to create a clear definition of what automation is. When you speak to people for the first time, you'll often find many myths and misconceptions that need to be debunked and replaced with accurate information. There will be some degree of truth in many of their misconceptions and others will be flights of fancy from the world of science fiction. So one of your first objectives will be to create a common vocabulary for all stakeholders to communicate consistently without the risk of misunderstanding.

Automation – a brief history

You can argue that automation has been around since before the first industrial revolution. In fact, if you've ever been to an RPA conference, the speakers inevitably begin there, but I'm not going to go back *quite* that far! I'm going to focus on two of the most important stepping-stones to modern day RPA.

Many IT professionals confuse modern RPA with a technique known as screen-scraping and, to be completely fair, there are many similarities in purpose if not in the method of execution. Screen-scraping was an approach used to extract information from legacy mainframe applications for use in other applications. Applications used computer terminals to connect to the mainframe; these terminals were sometimes referred to as green screens for their green-on-green or green-on-black colour schemes. As they displayed text only, a screen-scraping application would read each of the pixels to begin translating it into readable text that could be used in other applications. As Windows-based technologies took over, terminal emulators were created to simulate old-style terminals, so legacy mainframe applications still displayed as green-on-black within a separate window. Screen-scraping emerged as the integration layer between old legacy applications and modern Windows systems. If you've gone to book your holiday at a travel agent in the last 20 years, it's quite possible you'd have seen screen-scraping in action as it was frequently used to knit together the data from the various airline systems.

Screen-scraping evolved sufficiently to read both information from the screen and simulate user behaviour by writing information back. But the technology wasn't robust and some of the negative feelings towards RPA come from people who remember its original limitations. The resilience issues arose because the smallest changes in the underlying mainframe application could cause the screen-scraping to fail; the data had to be in *precisely* the same position on the screen every time for it to work. The fear of RPA solutions being fragile is still a concern today[6].

Application changes were less frequent than they are these days, so the solution worked adequately within the limitations of the technology at the time. However, small changes on the local PC, such as font or, window sizes and colours could all impact reliability! Despite its limitations, it met a need at the time and, was still a successful and popular choice.

Reading information from the screen like this continues to be a need for modern applications too, although the tech-

---
[6]WorkFusion Conference London 2018 – Fragility of solutions was identified as the number 1 concern by participants.

nology and the approach to achieving this has advanced considerably. Computer vision, as it is now called, applies AI technology to reading the contents of the screen in order to increase the resilience of modern RPA.

After screen-scraping, the second most important stepping-stone was the advances in End User Computing (EUC). EUC is the ability for end users to create programs of their own rather than it being the explicit responsibility of programmers in the IT department as it was traditionally. Spreadsheet applications and macros were the first steps towards end-user driven automation. Although their scope of operation was quite limited at first, regular mundane tasks such as reformatting data could now be automated using macros.

If you're not familiar with RPA but you know about macros in a spreadsheet, there are many similarities. When a macro runs, you'll see data moving from cell to cell as if an invisible person were operating the PC. The same is true of RPA, only now the "invisible person" can access information in *all* your desktop applications and is not just limited to the confines of a spreadsheet.

As macro-languages developed, these EUC applications achieved greater functionality with interconnection to other applications such as emailing or writing information back to databases. However, the resource pool was limited to a small number of power users who had the level of skill needed and the ability to understand and leverage the technology. The technology was also limited to only those few applications that could be accessed from the macro language itself.

Most modern automation vendors are the natural evolution of EUC; they provide simple business tools that allow consistent, repetitive tasks to be automated across an increasing number of different underlying applications. The genius of RPA is that it can use exactly the same interface as a person would use sitting at their PC. You're no longer limited to connecting a few applications but now almost anything that runs on your Windows PC can be accessed via these new RPA products:

- If you have a large list of files that need to be renamed, automation can now do this for you.
- If you copy information from your core customer system into your policy administration system, automation can now do this for you.
- If you have to collate information from several websites into a summary report, automation can now do this for you.

I'll be looking at many examples of how RPA can be deployed, so for now, if you imagine any repetitive task you undertake on your PC, it's probably a good opportunity for automation.

Definition

The term "RPA" is a relatively new addition to the vocabulary of automation; vendors have been developing the solutions for much longer than the term itself has been in circulation. It's hard to pinpoint exactly where the term originated although some point to the company Blue Prism as being the originators, as it referred to their specific type of automation.

Today the term is used more generally to define a cluster of approaches which automate tasks that would have been traditionally carried out by an individual. These tools use the same interfaces as people do; mimicking the actions of real people.

You'll undoubtedly face a whole load of misconceptions, so your first step to eliminate them is to create a clear definition and understanding of RPA. These misconceptions will vary: there are those who'll quote lines from The Terminator movies at you and others who have visions of industrial robots, the kind you see making cars, now sitting at a desk with a PC in front of them. For all these people, your goal is to explain that it's just a piece of software running on a computer that imitates the actions that are currently being undertaken by a person.

Once you've got over the first hurdle of Terminator myths, you can find a wonderfully succinct definition of RPA from the Institute for Robotic Process Automation and Artificial Intelligence (IRPA AI). This will help you get started:

> "Robotic process automation (RPA) is the application of technology that allows employees in a company to configure computer software or a 'robot' to capture and interpret existing applications for processing a transaction, manipulating data, triggering responses and communicating with other digital systems" [7]

Let's break this definition down into bite size pieces:

- The automation software is called a robot
- It will need to be configured to automate your processes

---

[7] Institute for Robotic Process Automation and Artificial Intelligence. https://irpaai.com/definition-and-benefits/

- It will communicate with existing IT systems, typically via the same graphical user interface (GUI) used by employees
- The tasks it can complete are repetitive and easy to understand

Classifying Automation

> Creating a **Common Vocabulary** for your stakeholders will advance your understanding and reduce misconceptions.

Now that you've debunked a few myths and brought everyone onto the same page, it's time to drill a bit deeper and explain that there are different types of automation available, suitable for approaching the solution and solving a variety of problems in different ways.

In this section you'll find real-world examples of how the different types of automation may look; this is the next step in bringing the IRPA AI formal definition to life.

Understanding the different types of automation will help people within your own organisation to think about how each different type might work; clear examples of the *art of the possible*, will allow your stakeholders to understand what types of problem each solution addresses best.

The different types of automation each have different levels of complexity involved with their introduction. The more complex business problems can be solved but need approaches that are more advanced and therefore more difficult to implement. When they understand the differences, your company stakeholders will be on the right path to evaluating the fit that is most likely the best for the organisation. At this point, I'm not looking at individual vendor pros-and-cons, (this is in chapter 4); I'm talking about building the common vocabulary needed to move on to the detailed discussions of selecting the right type of automation to meet business needs and selecting the right processes to automate.

Many of the suggestions you experience at this stage often fall into the overly optimistic or terribly uninformed categories. It isn't unusual for stakeholders to have grand ideas about automating processes that are either unsuitable or too complicated.

During a first meeting a client once suggested to me that they should automate a process that their own people found difficult and therefore they considered it the perfect opportunity for automation! This was overly optimistic and terribly uninformed because processes that cannot be clearly defined are not a great starting point for RPA. Equally, you need to remember that RPA is about the robotic AND *the process*; in later chapters you'll see that a strong link between business process improvement (BPI) skills and automation is needed for best results. Difficult processes are often just poorly understood and the combination of good process skills and automation will help evaluate even the most complex situations. Something that's really complex is generally *not* the right place to begin your automation journey!

Let me introduce the five different types of automation, one or more of which might be suitable for your business:

Office Automation	Attended	Unattended	Virtual Assistants	Artificial Intelligence
• Replacement of manual tasks with technology • Automation in existing portfolio of tools • Automation through end user computing	• Automation of repetitive tasks at the desktop • Augment end-user activities • Save time and improve accuracy on processes which cannot be fully automated	• End-to-End automation with no user involvement • Automates repetitive and clearly definable tasks • Tasks that are difficult for users to perform (Time, Volume, Complexity)	• Interaction via text or speech using natural language • Varies from simple FAQ-Bots to complex interactions • Virtual assistants can "humanise" the interaction with end-users	• Machine Learning (as opposed to programming a solution) • Processing of Unstructured Data • Intelligent Automation (IA) combines RPA + AI

Classifying Automation

This book focuses predominantly on attended and unattended automation, but it's good to have a broader understanding of *all* the types of automation and how they are interrelated.

Office Automation

Office Automation is the natural evolution of EUC I mentioned earlier; these are the opportunities that already exist in your organisation without the need to invest in additional RPA software. While RPA has been advancing over the last few years so too have many of the modern applications solutions, providing automation capabilities as part of the package.

This has been achieved in a variety of ways ranging from ground-up development through to purchasing or partnering with one of the existing RPA vendors. Pegasystems and NICE have both added RPA to their existing products by purchasing Openspan and eglue respectively. Blue Prism has partnership deals with Appian and Trust Portal; Automation Anywhere are partnered with IBM; and UiPath with Oracle. These vendors are adding RPA capabilities to the Appian, IBM and Oracle products through these arrangements rather than developing their own solutions.

The first test is to check if your existing software licensing deals already offer access to automation capabilities or not.

The second consideration may sound a bit obvious, but it's worth stating. If your manual process is *completely manual* and has no existing IT systems support, then RPA cannot help; it can only automate tasks where a person interacts with digital systems. There are a variety of modern solutions that can be considered to fit this gap, such as SaaS (Software as a Service) solutions or low-code development options that can develop new applications or even replace some of the legacy systems more easily and cheaply than using RPA. The option of using low-code tools to replace core systems is a bit extreme but the development time is so short that it may provide an alternative approach to implementing RPA.

RPA isn't a silver bullet to every problem either; you've got to look at your own circumstances and consider the different options before proceeding. I'm absolutely certain you'll have opportunities for automation, but it's still worth taking a quick look at your overall landscape before beginning.

Attended Automation

Many organisations begin with Attended Automation, also called Robotic Desktop Automation (RDA), because it runs on your desktop. The desktop bot interacts with a user, increasing performance by automating individual tasks; this is often described as augmenting the job or role. This situation is most similar to the example of macros described earlier where the users themselves launch the automation task when needed.

Attended RPA solutions provide the additional capability of triggering an automation when certain conditions arise, usually when the user completes a specific action. Triggers can be used to eliminate duplicate data entry: when a new record is created, the bot takes data from an application and copies it to a second system. It can also be used for training purposes, with prompts displayed on screen as the user navigates through the system.

The limitation for RPA is not having the information in electronic form in the first place; if this is the situation then the first step is completed by the user manually, then they launch the automation to perform the task once the data is available. In practice, the completion of the task becomes the combination of human and robot, the automation taking the robot out of the human elements.

Case Study - Pensions New Business

The most common opportunity for attended automation is eliminating duplicate data entry - I'm certain many organisations will be familiar with this situation. It's sometimes referred to as "the swivel chair problem" as users swivel their chair as they copy information from one screen to another. If you only had one core system that you enter data into, that would be fantastic, but the reality is that there are often more. This was the situation in 2013 when beginning the very first RPA pilot for a Life and Pensions business.

Data from a paper application form had to be entered manually into seven different applications; while each of the IT systems contained some unique data elements, key items such as name and address were duplicated across all seven applications. Desktop automation solves this problem by eliminating the duplicate activity. The information is keyed in only once by the user and the bot keys it into all the other applications. All this happens at the desktop with the user who triggers the automation and can even watch it complete before their eyes; they can then carry on with the next task.

When first looking at a process, you'll often find immediate opportunities to automate small parts of it (individual tasks). Putting these pieces together over a period of time results in the whole end-to-end process being automated. As you become more familiar with this and your understanding of its potential grows, you'll realise there are new opportunities for automation. Each of the individual tasks improves the speed with which the whole process is completed because when an automation operates, it also runs much faster than the human could have achieved. You literally see it fast forwarding through all the steps. It will run as quickly as the underlying IT systems can operate, so if you're running old and slow applications they will still run slowly and RPA will only achieve a smaller improvement. But if your technology is fast, RPA will run quickly and complete the tasks much quicker than a person would have been capable of.

By automating a large proportion of the data entry, eliminating the need for duplicate data entry from the user, we reduced the overall process time by fifty percent and it freed up their time to do other things. In this example the company was in a growth phase, so it was

> possible to increase the volume of business processed without increasing headcount. This reduced the burden and time spent on recruiting new employees, and, in turn, made further beneficial cost savings.

Unattended Automation

Unattended automation shares almost all the same attributes as attended automation with one essential difference: there is no person in the loop. In other words, it does what it says on the tin: it's unattended without any human involvement.

Before the vocabulary of automation became blurred, attended automation was usually called Robotic *Desktop* Automation; Robotic *Process* Automation was used to describe unattended automation. You'll occasionally find the term RPA used to describe unattended automation specifically, but more commonly it's the generic term that covers all types of automation.

In some respects, implementing unattended automation is a greater challenge because all exception cases need to be catered for, the process needs to run end-to-end (or at least to the next point of hand-off) and it all needs to be scheduled when to run.

In other respects, it's simpler; the exact environment is completely within your control and can't be interfered with by messy human interactions.

Think of unattended automation as the process running all by itself in a black box. The bots themselves still operate like a real user, interacting with IT systems through the user interface to complete the required task.

Some vendors focus specifically on only one classification of automation and others provide solutions that cross multiple classifications. Even if both attended and unattended options are available, it's often simpler to automate one task at a time until you finally reach the stage of being able to automate the whole process end-to end. At this point, you can move it from an attended to an unattended process. You'll need to think about the differences in implementing the two approaches but the fact that benefits begin to be realised early, and thereafter incrementally, is a model that appeals to many.

> ### Case Study – Out of Hours Operation
>
> A small retail business assembles bespoke items to order. They hold a small amount of popular stock on site but most items require the components to be ordered when the request is received. A new customer order triggers requests to several suppliers for the individual components to make the item.
>
> Most customer requests are received through the website, accounting for around 70% of sales. The store is open from 9-5, Monday to Friday, so requests received in the evening or at weekends are not processed until the next working day.
>
> An unattended automation now operates 24/7 and is triggered by the receipt of a new website order. Data from the customer request (website) is copied into the Order Management System and stock levels

are checked. If stock is unavailable or falls below the minimum, a parts order request is raised immediately. Finally, a confirmation email is sent to the customer.

Before automation, this process was the first task that had to be done every day. Mondays were the most problematic, as it usually took all morning to process the backlog of orders received over the weekend, creating a bottleneck in the process. The upshot of this was a spike in assembly activity on Thursdays and Fridays, when the number of defects (and consequently wastages) were highest as the team were under pressure to complete the assembly.

The introduction of a very simple unattended solution saved time, provided opportunities for growth, improved the quality of the goods, reduced overtime expenditure, improved morale and increased customer satisfaction.

Virtual Assistants

We interact with Virtual Assistants (also known as chatbots) using natural language. The advances in text and speech recognition have been astounding in recent years and Virtual Assistants like Alexa, Siri and Cortana all make natural language interactions more common.

The complexity of Virtual Assistants can vary greatly. At the simplest end of a spectrum you have FAQ (Frequently Asked Questions) bots which can understand your queries and provide a simple answer. You just speak or type your question and you get the answer you'd find in the FAQs on a website. This type of assistant can understand all the various phrases or words you might use so you can interact in a very natural way, but the responses are still single answers to a specific question. This type of virtual assistant provides a quick way of getting the information you want rather than having to search through mountains of FAQs. It's just a clever way to tap into static knowledge and it's now surprisingly easy to create and deploy these types of assistant.

Virtual Assistants are becoming far more sophisticated and can understand more difficult real-world scenarios; context is everything in this situation. Unlike FAQ bots which treat every interaction as new, Virtual Assistants can now carry out multi-part interactions that retain what it learned from previous steps. For example, if you ask about a train journey, as it learns more about your situation (current station, destination), it retains this knowledge as you advance through the dialogue.

More complex Virtual Assistants can interface with unattended RPA, returning information to the customer from a bot through the messenger window, or running an entire process requested by the customer.

At the complex end of the spectrum, Virtual Assistants overlap into the next classification: Artificial Intelligence. The bot can learn from the questions being asked and only refer back to a real person when it has an insufficient level of confidence to give the correct response. The AI element is the ability to learn from each response, which adds to its knowledge and increases the probability of answering similar questions in the future.

> ## Case Study – Wzard's Apprentice
>
> Simple Question and Answer bots can now be produced quickly and cheaply, by converting a typical FAQs into a format that a chatbot can understand.
>
> On my company website, the 1st generation chatbot was created in only a few hours. I didn't need to program in every question a user might ask because the ability to understand synonyms is part of the Microsoft QNAMaker[a] solution. It maintains a log of the questions and answers automatically and this gives it the opportunity to verify content or add new answers to questions that it couldn't previously understand.
>
> It's also relatively easy to extend these chatbots for use in third party messenger apps such as Skype, Slack or Kik.
>
> [a] https://www.qnamaker.ai

IA and AI

Intelligent Automation (IA) is the combination of RPA with AI. While AI is a separate discipline, you'll see in the final chapter how the two can come together to provide a comprehensive solution to your automation opportunities.

> **Google becomes "AI First"**
>
> In a keynote speech at Google I/O 2017 CEO, Sundar Pichai, announced[a] that Google were no longer a mobile-first organisation; they are now an AI first organisation. Since this announcement, the pace of change in AI has accelerated, introducing many new opportunities to automate increasingly complex scenarios.
>
> [a]https://venturebeat.com/2017/05/18/ai-weekly-google-shifts-from-mobile-first-to-ai-first-world/

AI is a huge subject. Strictly speaking it's a separate discipline from RPA but you'll see throughout this book that the two topics can complement each other and provide increased opportunities for automation. Academics are seeking genuinely artificial intelligence (see The Singularity[8]), but from a business perspective the term is used much more broadly to encompass an approach where machines can learn without the need for being programmed with the information (Machine Learning). A simple example of this is handwriting recognition. The machine is not programmed with every possible combination of handwriting from everyone on the planet, but is able to generalise an understanding of what letters look like by learning from many handwriting examples. It can then apply that learning to each new piece of handwriting that it sees.

In this scenario, handwritten application forms can now be read automatically, understood and the RPA will be triggered using this information. This is an example of IA:

---

[8]What is the Singularity? https://www.cnbc.com/2017/09/20/masayoshi-son-warns-of-the-singularity.html

the combination of AI and RPA. Without the handwriting recognition at the start of the process, someone would have had to key the information in manually as we saw in the attended automation case study for pensions new business.

There are two types of data - structured and unstructured. Information that is filled in on a form where the data is clearly defined is called *structured* data; this is a situation suitable for use with native RPA.

An example of *unstructured* data is an email message where the same request may be phrased in many different ways, depending on the personal style of the person who sent the email. This is a more complex example of using AI. The emails you find in a customer services inbox contain many of the same types of request, such as a change of address. AI can be used first to understand what is being requested and then to extract the data items needed to fulfil the request.

The algorithm must first learn what's being requested from a person. Once the bot has learned this to a sufficient level of confidence, it can start processing email requests independently using RPA to complete the task. If it doesn't understand the email, control is returned to a human user to evaluate; this action is monitored; the machine gets another training example (a process called Human in the Loop) and this increases the number of conditions it's able to recognise in future.

Many organisations are now applying machine learning to an increasingly diverse set of scenarios and they are only limited by the number of data scientists available that can develop the algorithms. This technology is also continuing to advance rapidly, providing interfaces to generate these algorithms with the need for less technical experience and less data.

Managing Complexity

At the beginning of this chapter I highlighted that the different types of automation each have different levels of complexity involved with their introduction. Simple processes can be automated using basic and easy-to-use solutions. Complex business processes can also be automated but need approaches that have advanced capabilities that are generally more difficult to implement.

The matrix below plots each of the types of automation that have been described in this chapter against two criteria:

- How difficult is it to implement? (the level of skill needed)
- How complicated is the process being automated? (the work complexity)

From this we can see that Office Automation and FAQ Bots may not need a high level of technical skills to implement and will only be appropriate for simple problems.

As you move from the bottom right to the top left corner, the solutions can solve increasingly complicated scenarios, but at the same time can only be achieved by a much deeper set of technical skills.

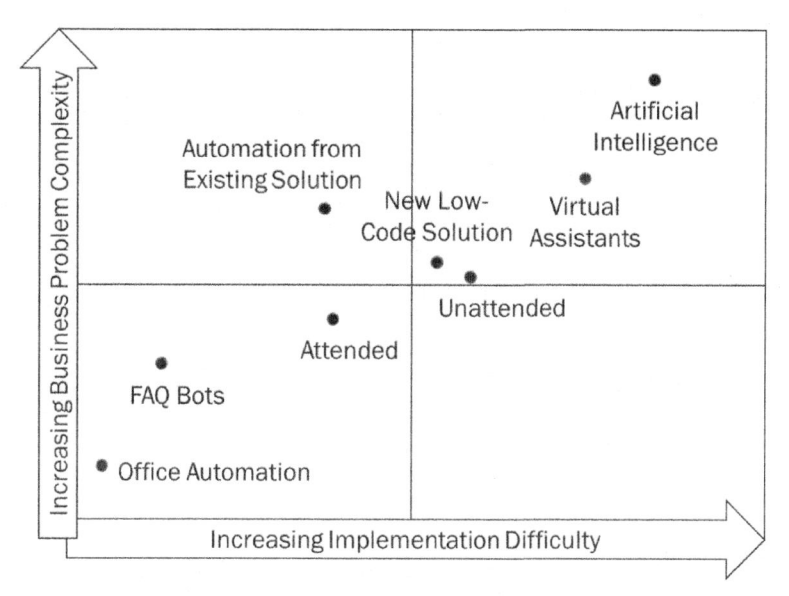

```
                                                    •
                                              Artificial
                                              Intelligence
      Automation from
      Existing Solution        •
                         New Low-      •
                         Code Solution Virtual
                              • •      Assistants
                              Unattended
              •
           Attended
      •
      FAQ Bots

    • Office Automation
```

Dealing with complexity

In addition to the classifications of attended, unattended and AI, this matrix also shows the sub-classifications described in the sections on Office Automation and Virtual Assistants demonstrating the greater breadth opportunities in these two areas. Helping your stakeholders understand these differences will help you identify the best approach to get started.

Exercise

Use your understanding of the types of automation to list examples from your own organisation that fit each type.

OFFICE AUTO:

EG - OPS KEY A CASE ORDER + FULFILLMENT CASES ACTIONS WITH NO HUMAN

ATTENDED: EG - KEYING ADDRESS CHANGE INTO OCIS + UPDATES MKCR

UNATTENDED: OUR MOBILE APP - WE CAN CLOSE AN A/C + DOES THIS FULL WITHOUT HUMAN IN B/GROUND.

VIRT ASSIST:
① BB EXAMPLE + HANDS OFF FULFILMENT TASKS
② SW FAQ CHATBOT.

AI: ① IF WE HAD A MAILSORTING PROGRAM THAT PICKED UP FREE FORMAT CHANGE OF ADDRESSES.

2. Why Might I Need A Digital Workforce?

Considerations before You Automate

The previous chapter looked at the concept of Office Automation. Technically speaking, this isn't a specific type of robotic automation, instead it's a view of related technologies that may be equally applicable to your own operating environment. We introduced several factors you need to think about before you start an automation programme:

- Are there end user computing automation tools already in use?
- Have existing IT systems introduced automation into their latest release?
- Do you have access to automation through an existing vendor (e.g. NICE, Oracle or Pegasystems)?
- Does your process use digital systems for input?

Accelerated Delivery

There are a variety of modern solutions which can also solve some of your automation needs. SaaS (Software as a Service), for example, gives you the functionality to deliver a specific business need on a pay-per-use basis. The growth of low-code development options (Mendix[9], Outsystems[10] or Pega[11]) offer a rapid application development platform; new solutions can be developed in this up to 6 times faster than traditional development tools.

---
[9] https://www.mendix.com
[10] https://www.outsystems.com
[11] https://www.pega.com

Low-code development and RPA have many similarities in their approach; tasks that previously took hours of IT programming time are simplified and delivered into an interface that's easy to use.

This creates an opportunity to develop new applications or even replace some legacy systems more easily and cheaply than introducing RPA. At first glance this option might seem a little extreme, but development using low-code tools is so quick that it becomes a valid alternative to using RPA.

Replacing your IT systems is no small undertaking but the advances in low code development and use of APIs are both increasing the speed of delivery. Be aware that introducing RPA may extend the lifespan of your legacy systems and that means you're more likely to increase your technical debt (the additional cost of maintaining them for longer than needed if you were not implementing RPA). Replacing legacy systems means they can be decommissioned and so the cost of your technical debt is reduced. The benefits achieved from the rapid deployment of key applications using low code development environments are a reasonable alternative option.

There's no doubt that RPA tools have evolved significantly over the last few years, but it's important to remember that your company may already have other development tools and software solutions that might be a better alternative.

The need for data before you begin

It's important that the quality of your existing data is good. Poor quality data or information that's only held manually can make it very difficult to get started and will stop you from progressing until you have a way to capture the information digitally in the first place. If you use the accelerated delivery options mentioned in the previous section, you can build and deploy solutions quickly and this gives you the opportunity to pull together the data necessary for future automation.

RPA undoubtedly has a place in your technology stack, but you should think about your wider technology landscape and business needs before leaping in.

Case Study – Q&A Knowledge Base

A Q&A knowledge base was developed to provide immediate access to information on common product questions. The knowledge base quickly grew to provide a comprehensive dataset on common customer questions.

The dataset provided several opportunities for the next steps. The base data could be used either for an FAQ bot or as the training dataset for an AI solution. Neither of these options would have been feasible without this source of electronic information.

The data was subsequently used to pilot the use of AI to respond to customer queries.

Reasons to Automate Now

Many organisations still haven't started their automation journey. The market is changing rapidly around us and well-known leading brands have disappeared almost overnight because they didn't keep up with the times. Technological change and customer demand are now the drivers that force organisations to look at automation as part of their company vision.

Blockbuster[12] video rental failed to recognise the new demand for DVD delivery and online streaming services and fell to Netflix. Kodak[13] actually invented the first digital camera in 1975 but held back from developing it because they didn't want to kill off the film business. Companies like Canon jumped in and Kodak filed for bankruptcy in 2012 after being in business since 1886.

If you're not already thinking about the effect these changes are having on your industry and your company, you could find yourself in real trouble as you'll be unable to react quickly enough to match your competitors who've already taken their first steps on their automation journeys.

---

[12] Why Blockbuster failed https://www.siamtek.com/why-blockbuster-failed/

[13] Independent – The moment it all went wrong for Kodak http://bit.ly/DigitalWorkforceKodak

The Future of Work

> Andy Haldane, Chief Economist and the Executive Director of Monetary Analysis and Statistics at the Bank of England, said that 15 million British jobs could be automated within the next 20 years

15 MILLION - that's an almost inconceivable number of people. So what does this mean socially and economically? If you're interested, there is now a lot of information about the social implications of automation. RPA is a key technology in the Fourth Industrial Revolution because of the social and political impact it's going to have. This won't happen tomorrow, but it *is* a problem that's bearing down quickly on us. It's going to impact the future of work and a lot of people are already starting to think about what'll happen as more and more roles become automated.

> According to McKinsey Global Institute, 60 percent of occupations could see 30 percent of their tasks automated with technologies available today

Job complexity is increasing across most industries; the jobs we expect people to do are getting more and more complex as companies attempt to match their business processes to changing customer demands. To address this complexity, the option to adopt RPA to *augment* processes will help remove mundane activity and can also be used to provide guidance to the user at each step of the process.

Changing Customer Demands

Surveys are a great place to start when you're looking at changing attitudes towards technology. What do customers expect from increased automation?

A 2016 survey[14] resulted in the following list of customer expectations, in priority order, from companies introducing automation:

- 24-hour service
- Quick answers to simple questions
- Getting an instant response
- Convenience
- Ease of communication

Customer demand has been changing rapidly because of the advances in mobile devices and it can be difficult for companies to keep up with these demands when their operating environment is based on legacy systems that have to be run by a lot of people.

If you're going to keep up with customers' expectations, you now have to run your business 24/7 and you must have a mobile-friendly interface to your services. Customer loyalty is directly linked to convenience of service; if your customer doesn't like the service you deliver, they just move on to the company that *does* offer what they expect.

One of the challenges companies face is the lack of application programming interfaces (APIs). Without them, there's

---
[14] 2016, My Clever Agency

no real time interaction with your legacy systems. APIs are used by modern solutions to integrate your IT systems with websites or mobile devices. RPA can become the interface that allows remote access from a website or portal. The robot opens new opportunities for your customers to access their data by acting like a broker between the portal and the legacy system (simulating how APIs work). It can run 24/7 and interacts with the legacy systems in the same way the customer does to deliver the information that's been requested.

RPA and automation tools will give you a platform capable of delivering those customer demands by providing a way of integrating separate technologies.

Delivering your Business Case

In many organisations the first question you'll face is "what is the business case?" The larger the organisation the more formalised the answer to this question will need to be. Time, cost and quality are three factors that are always under scrutiny in any activity or project you undertake. RPA can dramatically improve all three of these and that's often the reason it comes on the radar of business opportunities. These are tangible benefits (things you can count up how much impact they have), but there are also intangible benefits (things that are important but difficult to measure, such as morale, behaviours, or customer satisfaction) that can be used to develop your business case for RPA.

Many organisations start their RPA journey by looking at their own internal processes, for example Gartner[15] asked a number of companies why they had first started their automation programmes. The results were as follows:

- Efficiency
- Cost savings
- Risk mitigation
- Predictability
- Enabling best practices
- Scalability of processes
- Accountability

Many of these factors are interlinked but let's look closer at each of them individually as they will form the basis of your automation business case.

---
[15] Gartner December 2015

Efficiency

Efficiency can be demonstrated in many ways. For example, the time taken to complete tasks is reduced as a bot can run longer hours, takes no breaks and can be allocated to a wide variety of different tasks to optimise use. A single bot that is fully implemented will operate for 3 times longer than your standard working day.

Cost Savings

Although RPA introduces new costs (and they must not be overlooked), the savings achieved will more than balance this out. People and premises tend to be the two greatest operational expenses. RPA reduces headcount or, in a growth scenario, reduces both the cost of recruitment and the associated physical space used by employees.

A bot running 24/7 provides an immediate opportunity for benefit if processes can be reengineered to accommodate the opportunity for extended working hours.

Risk Mitigation

Regulation is a factor in all industries and a crucial factor in this is consistency of process. People are prone to make occasional mistakes but RPA will carry out tasks the same every time and it's this consistency that reduces operational risk.

Whenever there's regulatory change, there are always new challenges for operations functions, and this means you have to retrain and audit employees so they're compliant with revised operating procedures. Once automation changes have been made and tested thoroughly, they can then be implemented for all bots at the flip of a switch.

Predictability

There's no sickness absence with RPA and it doesn't need to take breaks or annual leave. It provides a consistent resource that makes planning, and therefore predictability, of processes more precise.

The data RPA gives on how processes are running is far more accurate and detailed than when they are operated manually. This additional information provides a wealth of opportunity for using BPI techniques to predict demand and identify process improvements to manage unexpected peaks of activity.

Enabling Best Practice

Best practice doesn't just happen because you're implementing RPA. If you want the maximum benefit, you have to combine RPA with a business process improvement approach. RPA programmes can be used as a way to implement best practices; joining RPA and BPI can deliver results which were impossible to achieve without significant expenditure on IT systems in the existing environment.

Scaling of Processes

Once a process has been automated, it can be implemented on as many bots as necessary. Scaling up your process can be as simple as adding new bots. Some automation solutions provide very flexible options, which allow scaling up or down based on immediate demand.

Accountability

Accountability in this context means clarity of responsibility and ownership at each level of the organisation. This may relate to specific tasks or specific outcomes. Larger organisations tend to work in siloes and here, accountability is likely to be weak as responsibilities are shared across several functional areas.

Introducing RPA forces organisations to have a clear line of accountability for any activity completed by a bot. If a customer transaction goes wrong then a bot cannot be held responsible, this must be a real person. Industry regulators have reinforced this point in their advice so organisations are defining their operating models to ensure accountability is clear.

Act Now (It's Survival)

This chapter has given you many great reasons why automation may be right for you. If you're still uncertain, then think of it as an act of survival. It's not too late, many organisations still haven't started to automate. But it won't be long before every organisation has a *digital workforce* that manages simple transactional activities and operates 24/7 responding to basic customer queries. If you haven't acted by then, you'll be starting a fight for survival. You don't want to end up like Blockbuster or Kodak...

UK Financial Services Context

The financial services industry faces many challenges: smaller margins, increasing costs, increased regulation, higher demands for capital retention, and nimble start-ups stealing away small pieces of business with efficient customer-focused offerings. It's a difficult environment right now and that's true for most other

> industry sectors as well.
>
> FS organisations have historically seen their cost base increase in proportion to their business growth. The reason for this is clear: the easiest way for them to grow is to add more staff to deal with the increased volume of work.
>
> Business growth in recent years, whether organic or through acquisition, has seen the number of IT systems being used to manage the business also increase. These organisations must now reduce their costs to remain relevant and financially viable. Many of them can only achieve this by employing fewer people; to reflect the needs of a slimmer operation, this reduction needs to be companywide at all levels, including support functions, such as HR and IT.

Organisations usually want to protect their staff and try to avoid thinking about downsizing. Putting your head in the sand means you're avoiding the reality of the situation; the worst option right now is to do nothing.

A few organisations are tackling the problem head-on: they engage their employees in the problem-solving process and reward their support by offering retraining opportunities both inside, or if preferred, outside the business.

Some industries have found themselves in a growing market where they have to get a lot more out of both available resources and space.

In some places, resource (population) shortages are so extreme, so the only way to maintain current business levels is through automation as there's no one available to hire.

There is some positive news from short-term industry experience though; when asked about headcount, vendors generally indicate that most organisations are not downsizing. This isn't true of every company but even where reducing the headcount is the only way to make the identified cost savings, it can be handled well (as in the cross-training opportunity example) or badly (little or no warning). I'll revisit this topic further on.

Organisations don't downsize because they want to, rather because they find themselves in a difficult situation and have to do it for the business to survive. It isn't an easy choice but when the alternative is going out of business, that's a far more devastating scenario and affects *all* the staff, not just a few.

Examples of Automation

I've covered a lot of theory so far and it's time to take a more practical perspective on RPA. To close chapter 2, I'm going to take a wider view of RPA to see some of the areas where it's been deployed.

Finance and Accounting

Supplier (Vendor) Setup	Sales Reporting
Payments	Sales Orders
Invoice Collections	Journaling
Reconciliation	Management Reporting
Financial Modelling	Capacity Planning
Data Collection / Preparation	Forecasting

Finance and Accounting Examples

Finance and Accounting (F&A) functions were early adopters of RPA technologies and it's easy to understand why: there's a high volume of repetitive transaction processing. F&A functions typically use end-user computing (EUC) tools such as Excel and this can result in high levels of duplication and increased risk of error.

F&A processes often involve excessive amounts of checking. This is done because of the high levels of manual processing which is susceptible to human error and costly rework. Process Optimisation prior to automation is therefore highly beneficial to eliminate checking steps that are no longer necessary when the risk of human error is removed.

Several vendors have strong F&A backgrounds and this puts them in a great position to provide value-added advice above RPA alone.

Introducing automation increases the opportunity for F&A teams to focus on customers and analytics rather than on repetitive and simple tasks which often take up too much time.

Operations

Operations are full of task-based, repetitive processes that make good candidates for RPA; this is the second most popular area for starting out on automation.

Call Centre	Data Aggregation
New Business Processing / Vetting	Claims Processing
Business Intelligence	Supplier Review
Change of Details (e.g. Address, Phone)	Product Queries
Email Enquiries	Anti-Fraud Checking / Regulation
Account Closure / Cancellations	Data Consolidation and Reporting

Operations Examples

Front office functions which deal directly with customers and clients have opportunities to use the entire range of RPA techniques to increase customer satisfaction. Providing out-of-hours responses through chatbots and unattended RPA delivers the level of service demanded by modern consumers. Attended RPA can provide timely information to call centre agents and this reduces call times and further improves the customer experience.

Back office functions that handle administrative tasks are a candidate for most repetitive tasks; many administration processes are frequently repeated and follow a straightforward set of rules. Attended and unattended RPA can both provide significant opportunities for operations teams, but you should also think about how chatbots can be used to provide rapid access to knowledge needed by many processes and deliver improvements in process efficiency.

Human Resources

Payroll Processing	Employee Onboarding
Time and Attendance Management	Benefits Administration
Learning and Development	Compliance Reporting
Personnel Administration	Recruitment
Service Desk (Ad Hoc Queries)	Appraisal Administration
Referencing	Data Entry Tasks and Reports

HR Examples

Human Resources (HR) typically have many processes that involve data gathering, updating and disseminating. They are also responsible for resolving the type of ad-hoc requests that can easily be handled by virtual assistants.

Automation will disrupt HR's role, not only in their own internal processes but also in their changing responsibilities in the new business operating model.

RPA is a disruptive technology; it allows more work to be completed with the same number of staff and removes the need to complete mundane tasks. This simple statement highlights some significant challenges for the future of HR:

- Reduced levels of recruitment
- Reduced need to address repetitive process-related questions
- Increased ability to support the existing workforce
- Increased need to address the challenges of new business models, ethics and communications

Information Technology

Installations	FTP Download, Upload or Backup
Email Related Tasks	Service Desk (Ad Hoc Queries)
Application Monitoring	File Synchronisation / Management
Data Migration	Application Integration
Proxy for Application API	Technical Housekeeping Tasks
Data Collection and Reporting	Testing

IT Examples

IT has been slow to embrace RPA despite there being many opportunities to apply robotic automation to tasks and virtual assistants to manage common user queries.

Several vendors focus specifically on IT-related activity. Test automation is not strictly considered to be part of RPA; it's a discipline that covers the execution of system tests to compare actual test outcomes with expected results to ensure system changes are working correctly. RPA tools can easily be used for applications testing but they currently lack some of the capabilities that can be found in a dedicated tool.

As with HR, the role of IT is changing but still forms an essential component of your long-term RPA implementation.

Procurement

Inventory Management	Supply and Demand Planning
Purchase Order Management	Contract Management
Returns Management	Supplier Review
Regular Vendor Certification Checks	Email (Inbox) Monitoring
Contract Checks	Vendor Follow-up Chasing
Data Collection for Information Packs	Security Checks

Procurement Examples

Supply chain problems can mean the difference between success or costly failure. The manual steps of reviewing, collating and recording progress are all great candidates for RPA solutions.

Contractual evaluation using machine learning is already being developed and this will give greater opportunities for future automation.

Exercise

The goal of this chapter was for you to understand why you might want to automate. Now that you have this understanding, what are your immediate goals?

Getting Started

1. UNDERSTAND VOLUME OF TASKS

2. COMPARE ABOVE LIST TO UNIT TIMES TO COMPLETE

3. AWARD EACH TASK WITH A DEGREE OF COMPLEXITY

   a) 1×2 = GREATEST £ OPPORTUNITY

   b) COMPARE AGAINST 3 TO UNDERSTAND LOW HANGING FRUIT.

6/12/2022

3. Taking a Business-First Approach

The next chapter takes a detailed look at the leading RPA vendors and their different capabilities. But before reaching that stage, you need to think about three important factors that will help you set up your RPA programme for success:

1. Assess your business needs
2. Outline a strategy
3. Prepare a communication for employees

The first step in selecting the right solution for your organisation is to understand the problems RPA can solve and the opportunities it can offer. A 2017 report by EY, Get Ready for the Robots[16], revealed that between 30% and 50% of initial RPA projects fail. One of the issues that is rarely highlighted as a risk is the selection of the right RPA vendor to meet your current and future business needs. The increase in the number of vendors has resulted in a market that provides wide-ranging capabilities, so a crucial early step for you is to match up your business needs with vendor capabilities.

> Vendor selection should be based on your **business needs,** not the other way around!

---

[16]EY Report 2017 – Get Ready for the Robots http://www.ey.com/gl/en/industries/financial-services/insurance/ey-get-ready-for-robots

As you would expect, every vendor's priority is to sell you their product so their sales pitch will emphasise their strengths, rather than making sure your specific business needs are comprehensively met. If organisations begin their RPA programme with a beauty parade (bringing in each vendor to showcase their product), they're much less likely to select the right solution. It's absolutely vital to spend the right amount of time assessing your business needs before prioritising your list of potential vendors and holding your first discussion.

Similarly, consultants want to sell you their value-adding services to speed up your RPA journey. There's plenty of information that's freely available and that will allow you to do this for yourself, but it is time-consuming. Reputable consultants should be able to help you tap into current market intelligence without you having to research all the vendors yourself. You may find that a suitable partner to help you navigate your RPA journey will help speed up your project considerably.

Assessing Your Business Needs

You'll need to take some time to understand your own reasons for considering RPA. These 6 factors will help you quickly develop a feel for your specific needs:

- Business outlook and expectations (motivation)
- Budget
- Type of automation
- Technology fit
- Business fit
- Orchestration of digital labour

An assessment of the landscape to match your business needs shouldn't take long. If you're working with a knowledgeable business partner, this should be days, not weeks.

Business Outlook and Expectations (Motivation)

What is your motivation for considering automation? Do you have very specific needs to address or are you just looking to find out what opportunities may be possible by using RPA? Your expectations of RPA will influence whether you take a long-term strategic view of the situation or if you're just interested in testing out a few ideas to understand how and where automation may work for you.

If you know from the outset that this is going to be a *strategic* activity for your company, this will increase the importance of developing a vision for the programme and understanding the impact on your organisational operating model. If you have decided that it's a strategic approach, bringing some organisational change thinking into your programme from an early stage will benefit your vendor selection process. I'll cover this in more detail in the section on Scaling Up.

On the other hand, you may be interested in learning more about the potential for automation, taking a more *tactical* evaluation. You're not looking for an enterprise level solution; you want something that will allow you to test your ideas locally. You'll find that some vendors provide enterprise grade solutions, others offer solutions that are more suitable for small and medium sized businesses, but few provide everything.

In a test and learn scenario, where a company is experimenting to identify opportunities, it's not unreasonable to identify a product that's suitable for tactical evaluation but may not be the end solution if your RPA programme advances to scale. At first this might appear counter-intuitive, why spend time learning skills that you'll abandon later? First, there are many commonalities of approach so, while the tools many be different many of the lessons learned will be the same. This approach is frequently used in IT projects that develop prototypes, the prototypes themselves are created using a quick and easy to use solution that provides the opportunity for discussion before the main project starts and work begins developing in a more robust tool. Simpler RPA tools are easier to get started with and can provide a way to demonstrate potential before beginning work using the selected toolset.

Are there particular areas of activity that currently need a lot of people to complete simple tasks and where is the largest group of them located? The number of employees associated with a specific area will often lead you to the areas you should look at first as opportunities to automate. Back-office operations and finance functions are commonly identified as early candidates for RPA.

When you have a good understanding of your own expectations for RPA, you can begin assessing how well the respective vendors meet those needs.

You'll find that there are vendors who provide strategic, large enterprise grade implementations, while others are more suitable for tactical and local implementations which may fit small and medium-sized businesses. This is the first step in narrowing down the list of potential products to the ones that will suit your needs best.

Taking a strategic approach to RPA means that you also need to develop a view of the anticipated level of demand, how many bots will you need? It's an extremely challenging question to ask at this early stage but the importance will become clear as you read the rest of this chapter and chapter 4 and begin calculating the software licence costs.

Budget

How much money do you have available? This factor alone may narrow down your search very quickly! The good news is that there are enough vendors available to provide solutions to fit every budget and many provide products with multiple levels of functionality that are available at varying price points.

Bear in mind that this is just your budget to get started, not the cost of scaling up and running the operation (total cost of ownership is covered in the Vendor Assessment section of the next chapter). The initial budget for setting up your operation and the ongoing cost of operations are both important figures to evaluate before you choose a vendor. You can clearly see the difference between these two factors by comparing the following examples:

- Vendor A has a low-cost start-up model. The first 5 bots cost £1000 each per year, with discount options that are applied as the number of licences increases. This is a flat rate model that will cost the same each year excluding any inflation increases written into the contract.
- Vendor B is a perpetual licence. The cost is £2000 plus an annual maintenance charge for support and upgrades that costs 10% of the original licence fee. The first year therefore costs £2200; subsequent years cost £200.

The numbers have been deliberately simplified for comparison but, over 5 years, Vendor A will cost £5000 and Vendor B £3000. If both vendors were charging for 5 licences, this increases to £25,000 for Vendor A and £15,000 for Vendor B, a £10,000 difference! But, this doesn't necessarily make Vendor B the right choice for you. If you're looking at a tactical solution or proof of concept just to test your ideas, Vendor A's low-cost start-up model would be less expensive as the solution is only being used for a short time.

At the entry level there are vendors who provide a free service. These services have limited functionality and there are constraints on the size of operation before costs are incurred but they do provide options for organisations who want to try out RPA for themselves. Here, cost isn't a barrier to entry for RPA as there are options that are free of charge and give you the functionality you need to develop bots for your own organisation.

Enterprise vendors offer RPA as just one of the services they provide. If you're already using one of the vendors for other services, you're in an up-sell situation where your existing vendor is likely to be looking to add additional services to your existing contract. This could be financially beneficial for you as these services are often discounted for existing customers. It may also include vendor support that will help you through the transformation.

Medium-cost vendors generally offer a tiered approach where costs and the degree of available functionality are increased along with higher licence costs. This is another reason to assess your business needs before looking at vendor options so that you don't find that business critical functionality is unavailable in the licence that's on offer. Having said that, it is possible to start small knowing that the product can deliver additional functionality later when you need it.

You may find that enterprise level vendors will charge you for running an initial pilot unless you're already a customer. While this may seem a barrier to entry, it is a compromise of risk / reward and the higher levels of effort needed by the vendors to meet the demands of large corporations. The costs are used as a confirmation that the purchasing organisation is genuinely committed to developing the programme of automation. There are a variety of ways to negotiate around these costs, the most usual is the pilot development costs are discounted from the final price when the long-term contractual commitment is signed.

Whether you're starting with no budget or you're prepared for long term investment, there's an RPA solution to fit all budgets.

Type of Automation

The first goal of understanding the types of automation is to get rid of the myths and misunderstandings about RPA. The second goal is to understand how these different types can be used in your own organisation.

Now that you know about the types of automation and typical opportunities, it's time to apply this thinking to your own operation. Which solutions resonate most with the executive team for the tasks you want to automate?

The most challenging issue at this stage is whether to use attended or unattended solutions. There are pros and cons on each side and, as many providers now offer both, you're never going to be completely stuck if you end up making the wrong choice. I tend to navigate a middle path on this question because my goal is usually to achieve unattended automation, but the path to get me there is by using attended automation.

The exercise in Chapter 1 was to help you identify potential opportunities for automation. If you're still not certain, the tactical *test and learn* approach to evaluate your needs is the way to begin.

Technology Fit

What does your current IT systems landscape look like? The combination of technologies you're using will influence your vendor choice. Old technologies, referred to as legacy systems, can be a problem if you don't evaluate them fully in advance. Modern Windows applications and browser-based solutions are likely to work well, but what hidden applications skeletons do you have in the closet?

The precise versions of your core applications software can be important especially if they haven't been upgraded for a while. Most mainstream vendors aim to keep their software running to the latest technology standards, but not all IT departments have had the time or budget to keep pace and you may find your RPA solution is only compatible with the more recent versions.

If you use virtualised environments such as VMware, Citrix, Hyper-V, etc., they may introduce technological challenges that will narrow the field of suitable vendors.

Another problem can be where there's no technology and processes are manual operations handled by employees unsupported by any applications. RPA alone will be insufficient if there are gaps in your IT systems for some stages of the process.

One of the activities you'll need to undertake is called a Proof of Technology (POT). This is a verification that the applications you use are compatible with the RPA solution. It isn't feasible or necessary to do this for every vendor as you can narrow your choices down to 2 or 3 by assessing your business needs first.

When you're assessing your business needs against vendor capabilities, a surprise or two can pop up. Some vendors are limited to mainstream technologies, and others provide additional capabilities to take different technical approaches to accessing the same user interface used by a human.

If all else fails, most RPA solutions allow direct access to IT systems using their Application Programming Interface (API). For older applications, this may not be an option that's open to you. Taking an entirely different approach, direct access to the database records is a possible option. If the situation means you have to take this approach, you'll definitely need greater technical understanding.

Business Fit

RPA has evolved as a business tool rather than an IT programming language, although this varies quite a lot between different vendors. It can be one of the easiest assessments to undertake when looking at your own appetite to develop the automation.

Some of the RPA solutions are more similar to traditional programming languages that your IT function will be familiar with. These solutions require the same skills that you would require for a traditional IT systems project: a business analyst, a solution designer, a technical designer, etc. The bots are developed in a very similar manner to computer programs.

Although these solutions need to be developed by more technically-skilled people, they also come with advantages you don't often find in business led solutions, such as modular design (making re-use and maintenance easier); segregation of roles and version control (allowing parallel development and larger teams engagement); and greater degrees of control over how the robot operates upon the existing IT systems.

This approach is more suitable for businesses that have a strong IT function and who will generally operate a centralised function for RPA when scaling up.

At the business-led end, complexity is reduced and the automation is developed in a similar way to a flowchart or a simple list of instructions easily understandable by business users. Logical thinking is still an important skill, but the actual bot construction is hugely simplified.

The needs of a *Digital Workforce* are more similar to the needs of a real workforce than the monitoring of a traditional IT system. Policies, processes, procedures, training, retraining, process changes, performance are all activities needed to maintain your RPA implementation, and business functions have greater experience of these than IT.

Finally, there's a third scenario where the development of bots is not expected to belong in IT *or* the business. Some businesses prefer to use a third party to be responsible for the development and ongoing maintenance of the *digital workforce* right from the very beginning. This situation has important contractual considerations in respect of Service Level Agreements[17], but whether you go for a technology- or business-led solution, it's more important to find a trusted partner who will operate your RPA implementation for years to come.

Orchestration of Digital Labour

The orchestration of work describes the prioritisation, scheduling and routing of work to employees. Work is orchestrated in different ways depending on the type of activity and size of the operation. You may have a to-do list at the beginning of the day to work through, you may take the next item from the top of your in-tray or you may be told your next task by the computer system as soon as your previous task is complete.

---

[17]SLA – A measurable commitment to the customer, generally time, quality or availability-based

As organisations grow in size and the number of processes increase, they often introduce Business Process Management (BPM), a system that takes in all of the work that needs to be completed and then prioritises and routes it to individuals in the organisation. It tracks work to ensure that tasks are completed on time and monitors the performance of the people completing the tasks.

As automation increases, the need for BPM in its current form will decline and the need for solutions that also account for digital labour will increase. Where BPM previously orchestrated work to just people, in the future there will be three potential ways for the task to be completed: By the person, by the bot, and by a person augmented by a bot.

With unattended automation, vendors provide the scheduling and work orchestration mechanism that directs tasks to the robotic workforce. This option is currently developing, with some vendors developing their own solution or partnering with other vendors.

With attended automation, the work is initiated by a person irrespective of how it initially arrived, which could have been a to-do list, and in-tray or a task from a BPM solution.

Some BPM vendors have already integrated RPA solutions into their products, while others have created dedicated partnerships to meet the need of directing work, whether to a person or a robot.

New orchestration vendors are entering the market; this allows work to be administered across several automation and BPM platforms and fills a gap where the available orchestration options are limited.

During the early phases of your RPA programme, orchestration of work is not a significant factor as the volume of activity is low. If BPM is already used within the operation, processes are more likely to be understood and documented, and performance data will be available. This information provides you with everything that you need to know about existing processes and helps you to quickly identify good candidate processes for automation.

When organisations scale up and grow, it's essential to manage the *digital workforce* alongside the human workforce. If you spend time upfront thinking about how this will work, it will save you a little stress later. If you already have a BPM solution, the questions are: how will it integrate in the short term, and will it be needed long term? If you don't have a BPM solution, the questions are: what changes will need to be made short term, and is the integrated vendor solution sufficient to meet your needs in the long term?

Managing a few bots across a couple of processes is easy to understand, but when you're managing 100 bots and dozens of processes, you have to establish the same organisational rigour for operations, training, monitoring and performance as you would have in place for your regular employees. This will require a fully functional orchestration solution.

If an operation currently runs 9 to 5, automation opens the opportunity for effective 24/7 operation and this brings with it operational and organisational changes. Orchestrating the unattended "out of hours" work will begin to release the full potential of RPA.

Developing Your Strategy

By this point, you've educated your stakeholders in RPA and taken an initial assessment of the business factors that will influence your choice of vendor. You've started to bring together the information you need to develop your vision for automation. You're still in the early stages, but that's fine, you'll add more detail as your knowledge increases.

It's time to think about what the future will look like and develop a strategy to help you achieve it.

A **visual game plan** is a technique you can use to help you define your automation strategy; it helps you define your goals and describe in bold strokes what's needed to achieve those goals. It's a very visual and collaborative approach and it should spark plenty of debate and discussion with your colleagues as plans begin to take shape. It provides a focus for communicating plans and getting feedback before activities begin in earnest.

> Collaborate on your initial **Strategy** using a Game Plan

Developing an initial visual game plan is an exercise that can be completed alongside initial insight sessions. This will help stakeholders explain what is happening and describe the bold steps that need to be taken to achieve the target.

When to use a Visual Game Plan

The strategy is the why, what and how of your automation programme. A game plan is a technique that helps you to describe and agree your strategy by focusing discussions on these important questions.

Developing a game plan is an activity that becomes more important when you start to scale up. If all you want to do now is just run a few experiments with RPA, you can put this off until a later date when you've increased your knowledge. Having said that, if you draw up a rough strategy early on, it will help your thinking and facilitate discussions with stakeholders.

A visual game plan is a great tool for encouraging collaborative debate for activities of any size, whether it's large or small projects and programmes; or long-term strategic direction. It helps communicate the bigger picture and is particularly helpful when starting out on your RPA programme. There are, of course, other techniques for developing a strategy and you can apply any of these to create the next level of detail if you need to when it's been decided to process at scale. The game plan is a terrific first step: it encourages discussion and helps educate anyone new to the topic, while still keeping the discussion at a high level.

In the early stages of your automation programme, a simplified game plan will help stakeholders understand the goals, steps, resources and milestones on your journey ahead, by answering the why, what and how questions.

5 Steps to Completing Your Game Plan

The steps to completing a Visual Game Plan

Game Plan Step 1: What is your target?

What is your primary objective? For some organisations it will be cost savings, for others it could be the engine for growth. Understanding your goals for automation will help you formulate a clear message and provide a "true north" which everyone can follow and understand.

How will you measure these targets? Your answer will help identify milestones and understand the critical success factors that will measure your progress.

Game Plan Step 2: What are the Bold Steps on your journey?

Establishing the bold steps on your journey will take you from where you are today to how you expect the future will look. What does that future look like? How will you measure its success and who will you need?

Automation projects generally have stages such as: Raising Awareness, Piloting, Process Prioritisation, Implementing a

Centre of Excellence. Each of these stages will contain a number of bold steps needed to achieve your target and help clarify the purpose to stakeholders and employees.

Developing a game plan is not a linear process, it's a canvas that you can structure your thoughts on, so leaping around between the various component steps is perfectly acceptable.

Game Plan Step 3: Who do you need?

Each step will usually need people to help you complete the tasks, at this early stage you may not know exactly which person it is going to be so you would record the team or the role that will be needed to complete this in the future.

Completing this step will help you identify resource gaps and highlight any specific areas that will be a challenge. If this is your situation, you may want to add *confirm resources* as a bold step essential to the successful completion of your plan.

Game Plan Step 4: How do you measure success?

Identify the major milestones you need to achieve and develop a clear understanding of when they need to be completed by and how progress will be measured.

Be as specific as you can on measurement and think about how the data to measure your success will be collected. What is a measure of success or failure?

Game Plan Step 5: What are the challenges faced?

This is your chance to kick the tyres on all your previous steps and document what could go wrong! This step doesn't stop at simply identifying the challenges, you also have to work out what is needed to avoid or mitigate them. All this is time-consuming but if you take action early on, you'll avoid problems in future and save time and stress in the long run.

Common challenges faced by automation programmes are lack of support, fear of job losses, loss of business skills, technology problems and cultural adoption. Your organisation will be up against these and possibly more, so it's important for you to prioritise the most significant challenges and set out how you're going to respond to them.

Team & Resources	Steps			Target
• Leader (Evangelist) • Process Improver • Business Architect • Technical Architect • Dev and Test • Operations	**(1) Raise Awareness** • Insight • Vision • Communications Plan	**(2) Piloting** • Select Vendor • Priority Processes • Verify Benefits	**(3) Operations** • Priority Funnel • Optimise Process • Delivery Approach	**Primary Objectives** • Reduce Cost Base • Improve Quality • 24/7 Customer Service
	(4) Business Model • Leadership • Centre of Excellence • Training	**(5) Systems** • IT Integration • Service Agreements • Security	**(6) Maintenance** • 24/7 Operation • Bot Management • Retraining	**Other Objectives** • Digital Transformation
Milestones:	• Exec Support • Strategy • Process Design	• Risk and Governance Sign Off	• TOM • Education • Skills	• Development • Testing • Quality Control	• Benefits Measurement Tracking • Exceptions Management

Example – Simple Visual Game Plan

As you can see in the example above, the game plan has helped the team explain why they have started the programme, who they're going to engage and the key steps they need to make to deliver automation. The plan will become more detailed as the lessons learned from the first activities are used to make the steps ahead clearer.

Setting Expectations

When I started out on my own automation journey, the biggest challenge at the time was trying to explain to people exactly what automation was because there wasn't much information readily available about it. Today there's increased awareness in the press and more negative comments, so you'll need to take time to think about the message you're going to give to your employees.

In previous chapters I've talked about how companies and customers view automation, in terms of both business impact and customer demands. In this section, I'm going to look at the employee perspective and develop strategies that will help you communicate your automation plans effectively.

Ever since the First Industrial Revolution, people have been afraid that their jobs will be taken over by technology. The press are always asking "Will a robot take my job?" and there are plenty of myths and misinformation which make people worried. But what really will happen? We know for certain that some jobs will disappear and be replaced by RPA; the question still to be answered is whether they will now be replaced by newer and better ones.

In a recent example of Business Process Outsourcing (BPO), many UK jobs were moved overseas but there was no equivalent downturn in the number of people employed. They were replaced by new and different roles. However, there's likely to be a gap between old jobs disappearing and new ones being created, and this brings us back to your specific circumstances. What do you think will happen to your existing employees? What you tell them about your expectations can't be either too pessimistic or optimistic, *you have to be realistic.*

The Impact of Poor Communication

The situations you absolutely must avoid are not communicating your plans to your employees at all or sending messages that aren't clear or are unfeeling. In the first two instances, the lack of information will be replaced by worst-case scenario rumours and this will make morale suffer and your staff will be much less inclined to engage with your plans.

When you don't communicate effectively with your employees, implementing any type of change becomes much more difficult. Poor communication has been a significant obstacle to the rollout of RPA in organisations that were looking to grow and where there was no risk of job losses. On the other hand, a large insurance company that was highly likely to lose a lot of jobs handled the situation openly and maturely. Employee engagement was maintained throughout the entire process because of the high level of consideration and support that was provided.

Preparing for Growth

Many early adopters of RPA realised that attended automation actually augmented the roles of their employees and that gave them the opportunity to increase productivity and grow the business without having to take on any more staff.

If a business increases its costs at a rate equal to sales then they have a business model that doesn't scale up efficiently. The ideal situation is to increase costs at a much lower rate than your increase in sales, thereby improving the profit margin. Unfortunately, traditional businesses tended to grow by adding people so the ratio between employees and costs remained fairly constant. Start-ups take a different approach: they can scale up by design, using technology to ensure that, as their business grows, the ratio of employees to costs increases and their overall profitability increases as a proportion of written business.

Small businesses often find that the expense of moving to larger premises is a barrier to growth. Automating mundane tasks enhances productivity immediately and allows them to continue growing their business while remaining in the same size location.

The message for employees is entirely positive: the business is growing, so there'll be plenty of opportunities for more interesting work.

Dealing with Resource Shortages or Fluctuating Seasonal Demand

Dealing with a shortage of employees is the complete opposite of most expectations of the impact of RPA but it's a real problem for some industries and locations. In Japan, for example, there is a cultural problem of overwork which is being generated by a shrinking workforce. RPA has been identified as the approach to continue operating at existing business levels while maintaining a healthy work/life balance for employees[18].

Industries that experience variation in seasonal demand are also faced with similar challenges, for example, meeting

---
[18] http://www.koreaittimes.com/news/articleView.html?idxno=77138

servicing peaks such as the tax year end or seasonal retail spikes. What normally happens is that companies overstaff and retain more employees than necessary during the off-peak season to handle the additional workload of hiring and training temporary staff to process work during the peak season. New temporary employees are inexperienced, so it is difficult for them to handle the high volume of work and deliver the same standard of quality as experienced staff, leading to rework and customer dissatisfaction on cases that have errors.

In the next chapter you'll find out which RPA vendors offer pay-per-use options. This licencing model may be more suitable if a significant volume of your business transactions happens over a relatively small part of the year.

Managing through Natural Attrition

Managing through natural attrition is a method of realising the benefits of automation through headcount reduction at the normal rate of employee turnover. This may or may not be an option, depending on upon your organisation's normal attrition rate.

There will also be an impact on HR as they are involved in recruitment, referencing and other employee engagement. The need for HR staff decreases as the number of employees reduces overall.

Redeployment and Reskilling

You'll find that successful communication of your automation vision engages everyone and gives the staff opportunities to be redeployed and/or to learn new skills. This ensures that employees are offered as many alternatives as possible to maintain continuity of employment. Redeployment and reskilling aren't limited to the opportunities within your own operation but also externally. A key element of holding mature conversations is helping employees get training in new industries and move on into other roles outside the organisation. New roles will undoubtedly be created within your organisation as automation develops and this will lead to new opportunities in intelligent automation. As the disciplines develop, there's also a growing need for new roles in data science and cybersecurity.

So, the short-term challenge is likely to be that the people who are most at risk of displacement are not going to be the ones who have these new types of skills; and that leads to a short-term staffing deficit. However, in the longer term, new role creation will be an important part of what happens next.

There's one really important question you must ask before you start your RPA programme: What happens to the employees? You must be open, honest and transparent about that step of the process and your answer must be clear and easy for them to understand. Explaining what will happen next and giving your staff expected timelines will maintain engagement and help the programme progress smoothly rather than generating a lot of fear and distrust that will inevitably cause issues.

Cultural Challenges: Trust vs Control

RPA technologies have matured to the point where they are remarkably straightforward to learn, deploy and scale. The technology itself is capable. The greatest barrier now is a lack of collaborative thinking and the fear of change. Even with a well-thought-out communications plan, the existing organisational culture will influence the level of difficulty you'll face.

One of the earliest challenges I faced from the stakeholders I needed to help drive the changes was one of disbelief. This position is increasingly unfounded as RPA capabilities are significant, but you'll still hear people say things like "Automation could never do my job," implying that their particular job requires a level of knowledge or complexity that machines just aren't capable of.

Advanced robots can exceed human performance when applied to a very specific problem or narrow field of study, for example, when Deep Blue and AlphaGo beat a chess grand master and a Go Champion respectively. This is very different to the business problems tackled by RPA; here we are looking at much simpler needs. Humans can become very skilled in a wide range of activities, whereas a machine is likely to perform better when applied to a narrow problem.

The good news for organisations that are highly controlling is that they're likely to be in a great position to begin RPA because their procedures tend to be robotic and very well documented. The bad news is that, of all the behaviours, this is the most difficult one to tackle when you're introducing RPA. Once you've overcome the leadership challenges of controlling organisations, you'll find it leads on to a second challenge: increasing the level of empowerment and skilled roles in the organisational mix needed for RPA teams to thrive, a difficult concept for controlling leadership to understand and value.

Thankfully not all organisations are controlling; many have worked hard to develop a people-centric culture, empowering their employees to collaborate on common problems and opportunities. In this scenario, RPA will be seen almost immediately as an opportunity to let robots deal with the mundane work, which frees up time for other, more complex, activities. Introducing virtual assistants and attended RPA into an environment like this, for example, is much more likely to be viewed positively. When boring, manual tasks are automated, the extra time gained will be an opportunity for further value-adding activity. There's no reason to believe that processes aren't well documented in this type of environment, although they're likely to be less comprehensive than you'd find in a controlling culture, so you'll need more time to evaluate and optimise processes before beginning.

Communicate the Goal and Impact

One of the first follow-up actions from developing your Visual Game Plan will be to think about the impact on your employees.

> Communicate the goal and the impact on employees **clearly**

Raising awareness for executives, stakeholders and employees brings together all of the topics in our first three chapters.

- Understanding what RPA is
- Classifying the types of automation
- Expectations (vision) for automation and its impact
- Everyone's role; who will be involved
- Expected impact on employees
- Feedback opportunities

Exercises

Complete a Business Assessment. For each of the 6 factors, document your business needs concisely:

- Business outlook and expectations
- Budget
- Type of automation
- Technology fit
- Business fit
- Orchestration of digital labour

(2) ✏️ Develop the first draft of your Visual Game Plan, covering the target (goals), bold steps, resources and milestones expected.

(3) ✏️ Write down the key messages you'll need to communicate to your employees about your automation plans.

(1) A — LBG:
  - We are set to automate more in the future & make journeys simpler
B — We will need clear benefits or non-starter
C — We have some fear of bots, so lets go for unattended
D — We have aging Bus Architecture, so this will be a challenge
E — We are big enough that we can find right area fit (Retail/IP+I)
F — We will need to overlay SLAs + existing expectations.

②

③ RESOURCES:
- PO
- ANALYSTS
- SMEs
- BUSINESS
- "TOOL OWNER?"

② HOW:
- Ⓐ COMMS ENGAGEMENT
- Ⓑ EXEC BUY-IN
- Ⓒ PILOTING & TARGET PROCESSES
- Ⓓ SYSTS. UNDERSTAND

① ‑ TO ENABLE GROWTH
↓ COSTS
‑ TO REDUCE HUMAN ERROR

④ MILESTONES:
- Ⓐ SIGN-OFF / INITIATE
- Ⓒ PILOT
- Ⓑ TEAM ASSEMBLED

⑤ CHALLENGES:
- Ⓐ CULTURE RISK

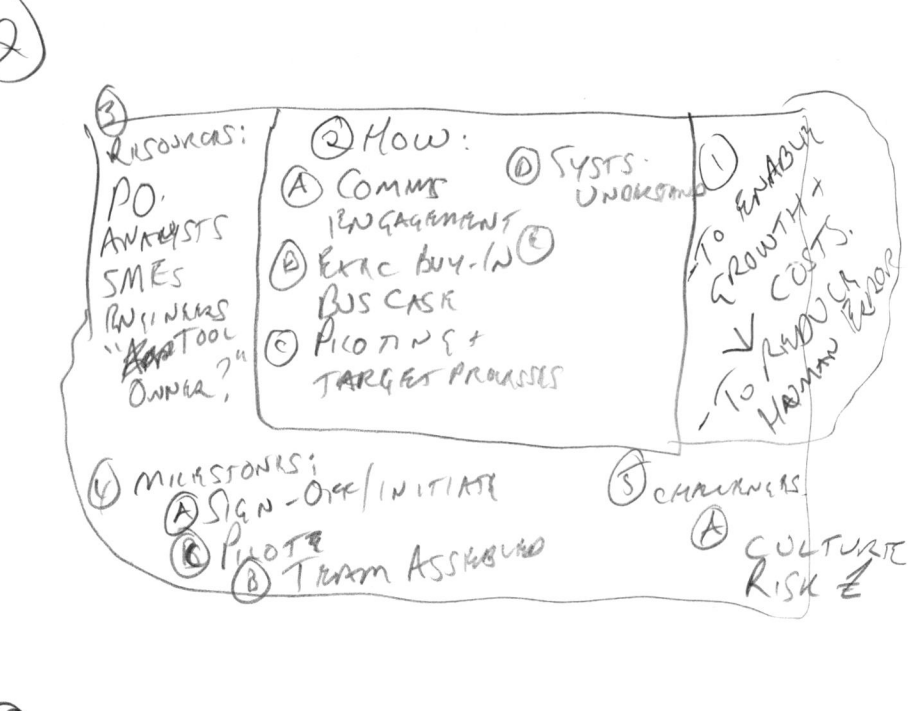

---

③

- NO JOB LOSSES
- THIS IS ABOUT GROWTH
- WE NEED YOU..... GET INVOLVED!
- USE TEST CASE FROM OTHER COMPANIES

4. The Automation Vendors

There are currently over 30 RPA vendors in the market and the numbers are increasing all the time. Their capabilities differ greatly and this chapter looks at how some of the most well-known match up to the business needs you identified in chapter 3. This will allow you to evaluate a few additional vendor-specific considerations before you make your final shortlist of potential candidates.

Various industry analysts have taken different approaches to classify and evaluate the RPA vendors. Horses for Sources[19] apply a similar model to the five RPA classifications described in Chapter 1. HfS refer to this as their Intelligent Automation Continuum[20]. This model has three components:

- RPA – defines solutions which deal with structured information
- Cognitive Computing – lists solutions that deal with semi-structured or patterned information.
- Artificial Intelligence – handles unstructured information.

The separate classification, or continuum, of vendors is an increasingly difficult model to construct; strategic partnerships and outright company purchases extend the range of

---

[19] Horses for Sources Research https://www.hfsresearch.com/
[20] The HfS Intelligent Automation Continuum 2017 http://bit.ly/DigitalWorkforceHfSContinuum

services provided making it impossible to place a vendor into a single niche automation type.

As I've said before, it's really important for you to understand your own business needs and therefore the types of automation that will suit your processes. The number of vendors that can satisfy all your RPA needs is increasing and this reduces the need for you to consider multiple vendors to meet all your requirements. There are pros and cons to taking a single vendor route over a multi-vendor route, but all of them must be evaluated when you begin to look at the vendors available.

An alternative, and more popular type of model, to the continuum approach is the traditional four box grid. This looks more closely at the current capabilities and strengths of the various vendors to generate a view of market leaders. There are variations of this model such as Everest's Peak Matrix[21] and the Forrester Wave[22]. These models enable you to compare vendors by evaluating the available functionality and strength in the marketplace. Industry analysts' views of the market leaders (Automation Anywhere, UiPath, Blue Prism) are remarkably consistent. Although they have differences of opinion about the rankings of individual vendors, you'll see the same ones identified at the top:

---

[21] The Everest Peak Matrix http://bit.ly/DigitalWorkforceEverestPeakMatrix
[22] The Forrester Wave http://bit.ly/DigitalWorkforceForresterWave

Tier	Vendors
Market Leaders	Automation Anywhere • Blue Prism • UiPath
Enterprise Builders	NICE • Pegasystems
Strong Performers	EdgeVerve • Kofax • Redwood Softomotive • Thoughtonomy • Workfusion
Contenders	Another Monday • Antworks • Automation Edge Contextor • Jidoka • Kryon

RPA Vendors

Market Leaders

You've most likely heard of the market-leading vendors, even if you're only vaguely aware of RPA. Advertising and general press coverage have helped to bring these brands into dominance. They are referred to as market leaders because of the range of features they provide and their market strength.

The business goal of current market leaders has specifically focused on the delivery of automation solutions. These businesses only provide RPA solutions.

Enterprise Builders

Enterprise builders offer RPA solutions, but it's not their sole business focus. What these businesses have usually done is buy an RPA vendor and integrate its capabilities into their own product range. Enterprise builders focus on cross-selling opportunities to existing corporate clients in addition to developing new markets. It's often difficult to see the specific turnover and sales figures for RPA, because the available data is for the entire business.

The target customers are larger businesses and corporate clients, although their product offering may often be a suitable technical fit for smaller businesses, their volume expectations exclude them from being a viable option.

Top Performers

Top Performers offer a very necessary choice in the market; they navigate their own distinct path and differentiate themselves from the market leaders in their price points, capabilities or approach. The top performers are fighting for market share and their own place up with the market leaders.

Contenders

The Contenders are the many smaller vendors in the market, that typically offer either niche solutions or ones that are targeted at a specific industry sector. They bring a depth of industry knowledge to the table as well as providing RPA as a solution. If, for example, your post room already uses a scanning solution for inbound post, you may find that your provider can also supply RPA capabilities, by using the scanned images as the starting point for further automated processes. In this situation, you may find that you can partner with a vendor who can give you industry-specific advice.

Selecting your Automation Technology

If you read about automation technology in the press, you're likely to be familiar with the increasingly recognisable brands Blue Prism, UiPath and Automation Anywhere. Each of the market leaders are focusing on establishing new corporate partnerships, all with highly recognised brands. This increases the level of awareness and introduces new customers to the opportunities of RPA.

By growing partnerships and increasing capabilities, vendors are matching up to the multiple classifications that I introduced in Chapter 1. While vendors rarely belong to just one single classification, at the time of writing, none of them operates in all of them so far, although the enterprise builders are getting very close.

Most of the vendors only operated within one category first off, which is why early adopters of RPA may have a couple of solutions. This will be a core solution that is suitable for most operational tasks and a second solution that is deployed tactically to meet a specific need.

A variety of company purchases and partnership deals have been struck, providing greater service offerings to customers and meeting broader demands. Here are just a few examples:

- NICE purchased eglue
- Pega purchased Openspan
- IBM partnered with Automation Anywhere
- Trust Portal and Appian partnered with Blue Prism
- Oracle partnered with UiPath

Assessing Vendor Capabilities

Understanding your own business needs is the first step in narrowing down the vendor fit; you'll now be able to compare your needs to vendor capabilities as you work through this chapter. Vendor evaluation requires two stages: the first narrowing down based on your business needs, the second generally involving direct conversations with the vendors or partners to assess their overall capabilities further.

Evaluating vendor capabilities can be time-consuming so it's better to shortlist your choices first. When you've worked through this chapter, you'll have a prioritised list of vendors that meet your specific needs. From this you can take the top few vendors from the list and ask them directly about additional services they offer and the level of resources available to support your progress.

In the context of a book, these factors are constantly changing, so this is where vendor discussions will fill in the necessary details for you to evaluate.

The factors to consider in the vendor assessment are:

- Total cost of ownership
- Training / resource availability
- Partner / vendor support
- Industry focus (case studies)
- Governance
- Re-use / frequency of change

Total Cost of Ownership

Total Cost of Ownership (TCO) takes a deeper look at how vendor licensing (and therefore costs) match up to your specific usage and budget. If you are thinking *tactically*, a short-term view may be appropriate. If you're thinking *strategically*, long-term costs will be more important in your deliberations.

Taking the longer-term view will make it easier to see how the different licensing models affect the TCO. For this reason, you'll need to think about what you mean by anticipated usage to help your decision-making.

When you evaluate the TCO, take a 1-, 3- and 5-year view of your anticipated usage. Looking at these three perspectives of your projected usage will help you to compare the different licensing models available. These are some of the typical types of licence models (or mix of licences) you may consider:

- Perpetual licence with maintenance. The costs are typically higher in year 1 as they cover both licence and maintenance but reduce to maintenance-only in subsequent years. You can buy additional licences as usage grows. This approach smooths out the costs over the long term.
- Subscription service. These are typically cheaper in year 1 but can cost more in the long run. It's usually easier to decrease the number of licences which you can't do with a perpetual licence.
- Pay as you Go (usage-based). Few vendors currently provide this as an option, but if the volume of business that you process is highly variable then this is a model you should consider. If vendors don't provide pay

as you go themselves, a possible alternative is to purchase the service from a third party.

Different models use different units of measure, so taking a short/medium/long-term view of total costs provides a useful comparison of the real costs incurred. Vendors often offer discounts for higher volume purchases, but at this stage you should take a conservative view when benchmarking them.

Training / Resource Availability

The general availability of knowledgeable and skilled resources on the market varies greatly between the different products and, most importantly, between different countries. Understanding the level of available resources in your own region is a starting point to understand how easily you can access them on demand. It isn't a deal breaker if you're working with a partner or building up resources within your own operation, but it should still be a consideration in your vendor selection as it can impact you at all stages of your development, from getting started to expansion and growth.

In respect of training support that's on offer, you'll find that each vendor has developed their own approach. Most of them provide basic online or classroom training, and third party training companies can also fill a need. If you expect to develop these skills predominantly in-house, it's crucial for you to compare the cost, approach and availability of training of each vendor on your shortlist.

Partner / Vendor Support

Vendors generally focus on a few strategic accounts and work closely with large consultancies to service the remainder of the major account market. You have plenty of choice if your organisation falls into this category. These vendors' costs are higher but they come with greater levels of experience, which is particularly important for global businesses.

Many more organisations aren't classified as major accounts, so in this case it's important to understand the level of partner support available for the technology you've chosen. This may differ greatly from one place to another as some vendors have much stronger market penetration in specific regions. Even if you don't plan to use partner support, it's helpful to know that support is available as a fall-back option if there are problems and this will inform your final decision.

Industry Focus (Case Studies)

One of the best ways to find out if a vendor is suitable for your business sector is to read industry case studies. Here some of the top performers and contenders step forward as they not only provide automation knowhow but also the industry expertise and services.

Industry case studies are a great way for you to find out if a vendor is suitable for your business sector. They showcase the automation knowhow and industry expertise of the top performers and contenders

Most vendors should be able to give you both case studies and (even better) reference sites that show you they understand the needs of your particular sector.

Governance

Although governance isn't a one-size-fits-all subject, there are solutions that will fit all needs. The solution you choose must be tailored to your organisation's specific risk appetite, for example, a small sales business has different compliance needs to a 24/7 trading operation. It is a vast topic and it incorporates elements such as version control of the robotic scripts and security issues (access controls and resilience to failure). As you'd expect, different solutions provide different approaches and levels of control and licensing costs will be higher for those solutions that offer the more advanced governance capabilities out of the box.

- Vendors that offer solutions with advanced security and control features tend to be more expensive but may offer a tiered pricing structure that provides a level of service to match the complexity of your requirements.
- Third party integration is also an option. This varies in ease of use and level of integration but incurs additional costs and means you'll have to engage someone, either internally or externally, to set-up and maintain the integration.

One of your key responsibilities during the vendor assessment phase will be to evaluate the level of business risk to implement *strong but light* governance. When you're carrying out this step, I strongly recommend you collaborate closely with your IT security team.

Re-use / Frequency of Change

When you look at the processes a business carries out, it's not uncommon to see the same task repeated many times for different reasons. The ability to re-use automation scripts for common tasks varies across the different products and generally takes more planning to implement.

Creating re-usable scripts is particularly beneficial if processes need updating frequently, which is often the case in businesses subject to frequent regulatory change. Reusable components allow the change to be made only once to correct all processes affected by the change, opposed to solutions with limited re-use capability which would require the updates to be made to several processes.

There are a wide variety of differences in how RPA vendors approach re-use so this is one that's worth thinking through as it may quickly narrow the vendor choices available to you.

- Solutions with limited re-use capability can be delivered more quickly but can take more effort to update later on if circumstances change. If process changes are infrequent or your level of technical and design skills are low, then this is a good solution.
- Solutions with greater re-use capability need to be planned and designed more carefully so it will take longer to deliver the first process. Subsequent processes that can re-use these common components will be quicker to deliver and later changes will far easier to achieve. If the frequency of change is high, this is an essential factor to take into consideration.

Assessing the RPA Vendors

This book focuses on the top solutions from the three main categories described at the beginning of this chapter (market leaders, top performers and enterprise builders). This information should help you understand the current market and match a vendor up to your business needs.

Market Leaders:[23]

- Automation Anywhere
- Blue Prism
- UiPath

Enterprise Builders:

- NICE
- Pegasystems

Top Performers:

- Softomotive
- WorkFusion

---

[23] The Forrester Wave: Robotic Process Automation, Q2 2018 "UiPath, Automation Anywhere, And Blue Prism Lead The Pack" http://bit.ly/DigitalWorkforceForresterWave

This page is intentionally left blank

Automation Anywhere

Founded: 2003
Headquarters: San Jose (US)
Type: Private
Website: www.automationanywhere.com

Automation Anywhere[24] (AA) is a privately-owned operation, with its headquarters in San Jose, California.

Automation Anywhere were founded in 2003 and is now one of the market leaders in RPA.

Their *digital workforce* solution is rapidly scalable and suited to small operations through larger enterprises. The solution is technically robust and, at the time of writing, is leading the way for scalable, high-availability, load balancing and encryption that's suitable for large enterprise-wide implementations.

AA's innovative capabilities are what make the company stand out from its competitors. Examples of these are the bot store (for sharing pre-defined bots that can be integrated into your own solutions) and the IQ Bot (for developing machine learning solutions).

AA offer a licensed model for attended or unattended operation, an elastic (pay as you go) model, or a combination of the two, meaning that licensing arrangements can be highly flexible.

AA's partnership deal with IBM is relatively new but has the potential to provide access to many of IBM's BPM customers, while opening new opportunities through IBM Professional Services.

---

[24] Automation Anywhere Enterprise https://www.automationanywhere.com/products/enterprise

More importantly, from a user perspective, the solution is easy to use. Bots can be written in a simple visual / scripting language that's easy to learn and suitable for technically-savvy business users or business-savvy IT developers. The ability to create reusable automation scripts (Metabots) has been implemented in way that is easy to understand and simple to change.

When you're looking at the business fit, you'll find AA is suitable for a wide range of scenarios.

Business Outlook and Expectations	Target audience is focused on strategic enterprise level opportunities, pricing allows for small businesses to begin with a single bot.
Budget	When working through an authorised Automation Anywhere vendor 3 bots are available free of charge for the first year. Thereafter moving into an enterprise licencing model. Licencing options include a pay-as-you-go model for dealing with peaks in demand.
Type of Automation	Attended, Unattended and Intelligent Automation
Technology Fit	Native windows applications and browser based applications. Computer Vision utilises Machine Learning to improve accuracy when dealing with virtualised environments such as Citrix.
Business Fit	Business Technology that uses a visual interface and scripting to generate easily understand automation.
Orchestration of Digital Labour	Orchestration includes load balancing of automation to facilitate peaks in demand and failover options for resilience.

Automation Anywhere Business Fit

In July 2018, AA announced the completion of a $250 million funding round[25], giving them a $1.8 billion company valuation.

---

[25] https://www.automationanywhere.com/company/press-room/6145-automation-anywhere-raises-250-million-reaching-a-1-8-billion-valuation-in-one-of-the-largest-series-a-financing-rounds

Blue Prism

blueprism
Founded: 2001
Headquarters: London, UK
Type: Public
Website: www.blueprism.com

Blue Prism[26] is considered an innovator as they were first to see RPA as a separate business need, as distinct from BPM. The company was formed in 2001, focussing specifically on what was then a completely new approach to automation.

Their solution has been developed as enterprise grade, providing centralised management of a virtual workforce of robots that's both secure and scalable.

The governance elements and auditability are both well thought out; they also offer enterprise capabilities such as load balancing, restart functionality and encryption at rest. Few other providers do all of this which is why Blue Prism has to be on the shortlist for regulated industries.

The company has a clear vision of what the product can, and cannot, do and market it accordingly to larger organisations looking for unattended RPA use. Blue Prism offers an end-to-end process view; work distribution and orchestration; queue management; and central control of a *digital workforce* of robots working on virtual desktops.

Eighty percent of their revenue comes directly from licence fees; they have a small professional services capability for strategic accounts but their main go-to-market approach is via partners. Licensing is per robot or virtual machine. With enterprise capabilities come enterprise costs so, as their focus targets larger businesses, Blue Prism is out of reach of SMEs.

---
[26] Blue Prism Our Platform https://www.blueprism.com/our-platform

Blue Prism have developed a partnership with Appian[27] to provide integration between RPA and the Appian low-code development platform. The partnership is a natural extension of capabilities for Appian and adding this to their portfolio has ensured Blue Prism remains a market leader.

On top of this, their partnership with Trust Portal offers a platform with an easy to use customer interface which can initiate user-led automation (this isn't strictly the same as attended automation but the outcome is much the same).

Business Outlook and Expectations	Target audience is enterprise scale customers, particularly those areas with high levels of governance and regulatory requirements.
Budget	Focused on enterprise scale operations
Type of Automation	Unattended Automation only, though partnerships with Appian (BPM) and Trust Portal (Web) facilitate broader application into attended operations.
Technology Fit	Native windows applications and browser based applications. IT Infrastructure is crucial component of initial setup.
Business Fit	Model Driven approach
Orchestration of Digital Labour	Comprehensive Unattended Orchestration and monitoring

Blue Prism Business Fit

Blue Prism have raised £70 million[28] this year through a share raise, giving them a market valuation of £1.2Bn[29].

---

[27] https://www.appian.com/news/news-item/appian-blue-prism-team-drive-digital-transformation/

[28] http://www.morningstar.co.uk/uk/news/AN_1516889792213853500/blue-prism-raises-gbp70-million-as-annual-revenue-more-than-doubles.aspx

[29] https://www.telegraph.co.uk/technology/2018/06/26/blueprism-hits-1bn-valuation-companies-turn-white-collar-robots/

UiPath

UiPath
Robotic Process Automation

Founded: 2005
Headquarters: Bucharest, Romania
Type: Private
Website: www.uipath.com

UiPath[30] was founded in Romania in 2005 and started out producing software development kits before moving into RPA. Their open platform is well-suited to complex automation.

A community edition of the software is available for customers who are getting started with RPA. It's free to use for companies up to £1m turnover but support doesn't come with it. UiPath also provide a comprehensive free training academy which increasingly makes the company the first choice for SME businesses and boutique consultants.

Their solution offers both attended and unattended options and the business vision is to place a robot on every desktop, augmenting human-led processes.

UiPath's open approach is popular with users; the design studio is based on Microsoft's workflow foundation; robots run on the desktop; and separate virtual machine servers handle management and control tasks when needed. Partnerships have been developed with a number of other providers to use Natural Language Processing (NLP), Intelligent OCR and chatbots, all directly integrated with Orchestrator.

UiPath is a good all-rounder as they have options for every size of business. The visual modeller approach offers one of the most rapid development environments, and this is

---

[30] UiPath Enterprise 2018 Release https://www.uipath.com/news/uipath-2018-release

well suited to tech savvy business developers. The trade-off for this simplicity is the loss of some of the deeper functionality, but this isn't an issue if you have development skills available in your organisation.

Business Outlook and Expectations	Primary audience is a direct market approach, beginning to develop a partner network. Product suitability ranges from a small businesses with a single bot through to Enterprise scale operations. UiPath has become a first choice of independent consultants, integrators and self-sufficient end-users.
Budget	Community edition is free for businesses below £1m turnover.
Type of Automation	Attended and Unattended Automation, flexible architecture facilitates easy integration with 3rd party tools (eg machine learning or chatbots)
Technology Fit	Native windows applications and browser based applications. Only current provider to focus on multi-tenancy operations.
Business Fit	Visual Model driven approach, easy to use
Orchestration of Digital Labour	Orchestration included

UiPath Business Fit

In March 2018, UiPath raised a $153 million Series B funding[31], followed in September by a further $225 million Series C funding[32], resulting in a currently market leading valuation of $3Bn.

---

[31] https://www.uipath.com/press-room/uipath-raises-153-million-series-b
[32] https://www.businesswire.com/news/home/20180918005261/en/CORRECTING-REPLACING-UiPath-Raises-225-Million-Series

NICE

Founded: 1986
Headquarters: Raanana, Israel
Type: Public
Website: www.nice.com

NICE is a leading provider of cloud and on-premises enterprise software solutions that are used in more than 150 countries by over 25,000 organisations, including over 85 of the Fortune 100 companies[33].

NICE is a billion dollar plus organisation which entered the RPA market in 2010 with the acquisition of eglue[34], an early Israeli RPA start-up. They provide attended and unattended RPA, virtual assistants, cognitive, AI and automation finder solutions. Their business focus is call centres and back-office functions where their broader software offering is strongest.

NICE has predominately sold its solutions to its existing customers but has recently adopted a strategy to operate RPA as an independent capability and promote it more actively to new customers.

NICE provide the largest installation of RPA for HMRC in the UK, operating 10,000 robots across 57 processes. NICE have a 15-year track record of automation, making them perhaps one of the longest standing RPA providers.

Although the solution is technically scalable from small business through to large enterprise, the technical nature of the development environment is more suited to medium and large technologically savvy businesses. So, if you want

---

[33] NICE https://www.nice.com
[34] https://www.jpost.com/Business/Business-News/Nice-Systems-buys-eglue-for-29m

to exploit the additional control over the operating environment, it's possible through the NICE platform.

Although the NICE solution is more technical than all the other examples in this book, it's well suited to multi-disciplinary teams working in parallel on different elements of development. Skilled solution designers and developers familiar with object-based design are needed to deliver the best results.

Software updates are less frequent than with other vendors and this can lead to times when they're slow to integrate new functionality released by core software providers.

When you're thinking about the business fit, NICE is suitable both for the more technically savvy operation and for anyone who wants to have a greater level of control over the operating environment.

Business Outlook and Expectations	Target audience is a combination of existing NICE customers who utilise their existing call centre and telecoms solutions, and new customers looking to engage RPA for the first time. While predominantly focused on larger scale implementations directly or medium scale through partnerships. NICE is the software behind the HMRC Implementation in the UK.
Budget	Traditional software licencing model which provides the option of a competitively priced start-up.
Type of Automation	Attended and Unattended operations, basic Intelligent automation services are being integrated into solution. Attended automation is stronger than most with ability to manipulate activity to a very granular level. Product releases are infrequent.
Technology Fit	Native windows applications and browser based applications.
Business Fit	Object oriented design approach requires a good solution design skills, separation of work elements facilitates multi-team operations. Although largely interface driven, coding skills are needed.
Orchestration of Digital Labour	Orchestration of attended and unattended activities.

NICE Business Fit

Pegasystems

Founded: 1983
Headquarters: Cambridge (US)
Type: Public
Website: www.pega.com

Pega[35] are a market-leading provider of case management and customer relationship management solutions. In 2016, they acquired Openspan, an industry pioneer in automation technologies. This immediately enhanced their BPM offering, delivering the orchestration between both robots and humans.

Pega offers attended and unattended automation solutions, virtual assistance and machine learning capabilities, all of which are also integrated into their BPM platform.

Pega's business focus is generally on large enterprise. Their approach is to release value quickly through straightforward automation opportunities and then deploy the Workforce Intelligence (WFI) solution to identify further improvement and automation potential. WFI bots run on the user desktop and use machine learning.

Their wider suite of tools offers chatbot and cognitive capabilities in addition to the core attended and unattended bots. Pega provides a one-stop shop for enterprise level intelligent automation, in combination with low-code development and BPM capabilities.

---

[35] Pega Platform https://www1.pega.com/products/pega-platform

Business Outlook and Expectations	Target audience is a combination of existing Pega customers who utilise their existing BPM solution, and new customers looking to engage RPA for the first time. Focus is on larger customers working alongside key consulting partners
Budget	Pricing is geared towards enterprise customers
Type of Automation	Attended and Unattended operations, integration with Pega provides BPM process orchestration, native AI capabilities, predictive analytics and chatbot solution.
Technology Fit	Native windows applications and browser based applications.
Business Fit	Integrated with Pega suite, the RPA element is a model driven approach. Work Force Intelligence (WFI) provides an AI assisted guide to areas of process optimisation and improvement.
Orchestration of Digital Labour	Extensive BPM environment provides a view across both automated (unattended), attended and purely manual processes.

Pegasystems Business Fit

Softomotive

Founded: 2005
Headquarters: Athens, Greece
Type: Private
Website: www.softomotive.com

Softomotive[36] are a Greek company, founded in Athens in 2005. They offer a solution that targets organisations that want to start small and deliver benefits quickly.

Softomotive have two product lines:

- WinAutomation which provides attended automation.
- ProcessRobot which requires server-based authentication (Active Directory) to operate with the facility for attended (Side Bot) and unattended (Solo Bot) automation.

WinAutomation is a simple automation solution that's competitively priced. The licensing arrangements are per user, with three levels of capabilities, each providing increasingly more advanced functionality. The single perpetual licence makes WinAutomation a competitive option and is often adopted by small businesses alongside the implementation of a scale automation solution.

It's easy to develop automation scripts using WinAutomation and is well suited to business users who want to automate repetitive tasks. Desktop installation is simple and you don't need any additional IT skills which makes it a suitable option for organisations that have little IT support.

WinAutomation isn't a scalable solution but it *is* very cost effective and sufficiently powerful for many business needs.

---

[36] https://www.softomotive.com/

The product doesn't give you the level of control that's available in other solutions but it's well regarded in the industry, easy to use and allows your programme to develop quickly by simplifying many tasks.

ProcessRobot is a recent addition to the Softomotive offering. It uses the same development approach to creating automation scripts which can now be run as attended or unattended. Licensing is renewable annually. Development use remains simple, but set-up and configuration for authentication and *digital workforce* orchestration requires a level of technical IT skills.

It's theoretically possible to scale with ProcessRobot but as it only came onto the market relatively recently, it's too soon to evaluate it properly.

Business Outlook and Expectations	Small business focus. WinAutomation is also used in addition to other solutions at enterprise level to deliver simple desktop automation. Process Robot is focused on organisations looking to scale up from the attended option.
Budget	Pricing is tiered with additional functionality available at each tier. The pricing is geared towards small and medium businesses and can start as small a single desktop licence.
Type of Automation	WinAutomation is Attended only, Process Robot provides Attended (SideBot), Unattended (SoloBot) and Scheduling software.
Technology Fit	Native windows applications and browser based applications. ProcessRobot configuration requires integration with Active Directory, necessitating experienced IT resources for setup.
Business Fit	Deployment and Bot development is a simplified visual scripting solution utilisable by any level of user.
Orchestration of Digital Labour	Simple Automation Scheduler included with Process Robot

Softomotive Business Fit

In September 2018, Softomotive confirmed a £25m Series A funding[37] and plans to move their headquarters to London.

---

[37] https://www.businesswire.com/news/home/20180927005832/en/Softomotive-Raises-25m-Relocates-UK-Base-Global

WorkFusion

WorkFusion

Founded: 2010
Headquarters: New York, USA
Type: Private
Website: www.workfusion.com

WorkFusion is used by over 30,000 people from 10,000 companies around the world and is the most widely adopted AI automation product on the market. Both large and small companies can start their automation journey with free-to-use RPA Express, then, using WorkFusion's flagship product, Smart Process Automation[38] (SPA) they can grow their capabilities to solve even the most challenging work scalability problems.

Unlike other RPA vendors who are only now moving into developing their AI capabilities, WorkFusion started developing their AI capabilities first[39] and only moved into RPA in 2014. The SPA product provides a comprehensive and scalable solution for RPA which includes their Intelligent Automation components.

Another differentiator for WorkFusion is their approach to orchestration which takes a page from the BPM playbook and provides the ability to schedule work for both the digital and human workforce.

Their second product, RPA Express, delivers limited functionality for RPA free of charge, but without any of the AI capabilities included.

---

[38] WorkFusion Smart Process Automation https://www.workfusion.com/smart-process-automation-spa/
[39] https://www.workfusion.com/company/

Business Outlook and Expectations	Target audience is large domestic US enterprises with revenues in excess of $1bn. Development of the free RPA express product is to provide a future gateway into SPA.
Budget	RPA Express is provided free of charge with limited functionality. Workfusion Smart Process Automation (SPA) is the enterprise solution
Type of Automation	RPA Express is a simple attended solution. SPA is predominantly an unattended intelligent automation solution, though also provides attended operations.
Technology Fit	Native windows applications and browser based applications. SPA includes the Intelligent elements.
Business Fit	Visual Model driven approach, easy to use
Orchestration of Digital Labour	Orchestration included with a goal to orchestrate tasks between manual (human) and robotic.

WorkFusion Business Fit

In May 2018, WorkFusion announced a further $50m of funding[40] specifically to enhance their machine learning capabilities.

---

[40] https://www.workfusion.com/news/workfusion-expands-50-million-series-e-round-adds-guardian-newyork-presbyterian-the-pnc-financial-services-group-and-ai-capital-as-strategic-investors/

Other Vendors

It's quite possible that you've heard of other vendors that don't share the spotlight with the market leaders; they often have strong reputations in specific sectors. Kofax[41] and Redwood[42] are two examples of this type of vendor. Kofax is an established provider of post room solutions such as scanning and OCR, and Redwood have reputation in finance and accounting functions. Both vendors bring a strength of integration and knowledge in their specific sectors.

---

[41] https://www.kofax.com/products/robotic-process-automation/kapow/overview

[42] https://www.redwood.com/

Do I need a Partner?

Technically the answer is no, you don't. When you're choosing a vendor, there's usually enough information available to enable you to take on the challenge without partner support.

Having said that, there *are* many advantages to joining forces with a partner, particularly in the early stages (setting you up for success is covered in the next chapter). The major advantages are:

- Accelerating your knowledge and understanding
- Avoiding common pitfalls
- Helping with cultural challenges and hurdles
- Understanding future potential and the art of the possible
- Implementing the structure that will provide greater chance of success

Example Scenarios for Shortlisting Vendors

In this section, you'll find three hypothetical scenarios I've created to highlight different business needs. You can then evaluate the vendor capabilities against these to build a shortlist of potential solution providers.

Scenario 1

The subject of this scenario is a global enterprise with a major brand that has over 20,000 employees worldwide. They have previously investigated RPA and have now decided that it is a strategic objective.

They found it difficult to realise small incremental benefits in previous improvement programmes and are now in favour of unattended operation so that work can be completely ringfenced and transitioned to the *digital workforce*. The work they want to automate is high value and mission critical so they're looking to work with financially stable RPA providers who have major partners they can use for additional skills and resources if needed. The solution should provide high availability (99.99% availability) and 24/7 operations.

Scenario 1 — A global enterprise with over 20K staff worldwide. A major brand that has previously investigated RPA and now decided it is a strategic objective.

Business Outlook and Expectations	Strategic	Total Cost of Ownership	Perpetual Licence fits well
Budget	Strategic Investment Budget Assigned	Training / Vendor Support	Utilising major partner to support implementation
Type of Automation	Unattended is most likely	Industry Focus	Partner provides industry and vendor focus. High regulatory environment.
Technology Fit	Wide Mix of Tech, including out of maintenance legacy systems	Governance	Mission critical processes that run at high volume. Time dependant processes requiring high availability.
Business Fit	Building in-house team.	Reuse / Frequency of Change	High frequency of change (compliance and regulation). Ease of reuse is important.
Orchestration of Digital Labour	High volume; orchestration essential		

Scenario 1 – Large Enterprise

Shortlist:

- Automation Anywhere
- Blue Prism
- NICE
- Pega

All the shortlisted options provide enterprise grade capabilities suitable for this scenario. The potential size of the contract gives them an opportunity to negotiate on price and this is likely to be the final deciding factor.

Scenario 2

In this scenario, the subject is a medium sized business with 200 employees. They are looking to improve efficiency and reduce costs to remain competitive in a challenging marketplace.

Scenario 2	A medium sized business with 200 staff, looking to improve efficiency and reduce costs in order to remain competitive in the marketplace.		
Business Outlook and Expectations	Urgent tactical but open to strategic view	Total Cost of Ownership	Lower long-term costs will improve ROI and deliver cost reduction goal more quickly.
Budget	Small budget available	Training / Vendor Support	Looking for partner support to provide technical skills so need for regional vendor support is low.
Type of Automation	Attended	Industry Focus	Partner with industry knowledge may be beneficial
Technology Fit	Legacy, Citrix, windows and browser based. Existing NICE telephony user	Governance	Partner provided
Business Fit	Limited IT resource so looking to partnership	Reuse / Frequency of Change	Medium frequency of change
Orchestration of Digital Labour	None identified		

Scenario 2 – Medium Sized Business

Shortlist:

- Automation Anywhere
- UiPath
- NICE
- Softomotive (outside choice)

This is a deliberately confusing situation. The urgent tactical need might suggest solutions like Softomotive could be an option. A POT would be needed to validate this option in this complex legacy and Citrix setup.

Automation Anywhere and UiPath provide the right balance of scale, ease of use and operational capabilities, so either of these is the most likely choice. As previously, a POT would give the level of detail they needed to make the best choice.

NICE is a wildcard option, but the inclusion of a partner with an existing relationship is worthy of further investigation.

Scenario 3

The subject of the final scenario is a small 3-person business looking for opportunities to increase their customer base.

Scenario 3 — A small 3 person business looking for opportunities to increase customer base

Business Outlook and Expectations	Investigative opportunity	Total Cost of Ownership	Low cost start option
Budget	Limited funding available	Training / Vendor Support	Utilise free online training and select based on ease of use
Type of Automation	Attended and Unattended likely	Industry Focus	N/A
Technology Fit	2-3 core systems, all browser based, plus MS Office	Governance	N/A
Business Fit	Everything handled by business team who are reasonably tech savvy	Reuse / Frequency of Change	Low
Orchestration of Digital Labour	Low volume but some 24/7 operation opportunities		

Scenario 3 – Small Operation

Shortlist:

- Softomotive
- UiPath
- WorkFusion RPA Express

These options all provide low cost starts and are easy for business people to learn. There's no known complexity in the operating environment and the three shortlisted options all meet the needs of this scenario.

The decision-making process doesn't need to be complicated, so, in this scenario, carrying out a POT would be overkill for such a simple setup. Watching demonstrations of the three products in action should be enough to identify the option that best fits the business needs.

Exercises

- For each vendor, score each of your business needs on how well the vendor provides a solution. Rank them in order of Good Fit, Potential Fit and Poor Fit.

- For vendors that are mostly a Good Fit, identify the performance of those within your region (total cost of ownership; training and resource availability; partner or vendor support level; case studies applicable to your industry).

5. Getting Started with a Pilot

This chapter structures what you've learned so far and will help you develop a plan to deliver your first automation. To summarise what we've understood from the first four chapters:

- What is RPA, and, why might you want it (chapters 1 and 2)
- Taking a business first approach to evaluating your specific need for RPA (chapter 3)
- A view of the key vendors in the RPA market to match against your business needs (chapter 4)

You're now ready to shortlist vendors who meet your needs and to begin evaluating the wider capabilities of the ones you've shortlisted.

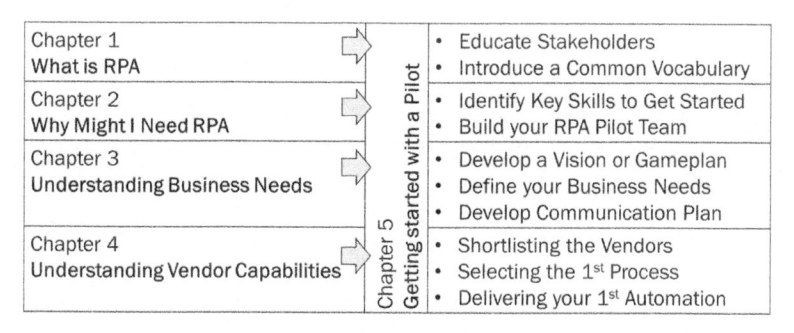

Chapter 1 What is RPA	⇨	• Educate Stakeholders • Introduce a Common Vocabulary
Chapter 2 Why Might I Need RPA	⇨	• Identify Key Skills to Get Started • Build your RPA Pilot Team
Chapter 3 Understanding Business Needs	⇨	• Develop a Vision or Gameplan • Define your Business Needs • Develop Communication Plan
Chapter 4 Understanding Vendor Capabilities	⇨	• Shortlisting the Vendors • Selecting the 1st Process • Delivering your 1st Automation

Chapter 5 Structure

Previous chapters explained the techniques needed to get started on your RPA programme. In this chapter you'll see how putting those techniques together creates a framework for delivering your first automated process.

Pioneering Phase

There are three distinct phases of activity you'll go through as your automation learning matures. The first phase is known as the *pioneering phase*; following this you begin to *scale up*; and then you move into the final *transformation* phase. The pioneering phase helps you get started - you're like a pioneer in the Gold Rush era of the old Wild West, trekking into new and undiscovered country.

> **Pioneering** is about developing, exploring and incubating ideas.

- Ideation: Before you can start developing ideas, you'll need to create the kind of environment that will foster innovative thinking. In other words, you need to start making the cultural changes that will help you implement your RPA programme successfully.
- Exploration: The exploration stage is when you choose an automation vendor, partner and toolkit. You may have to test one or two RPA solutions to see which one is the best fit and you'll have to learn new tools and techniques to apply RPA to your programme.
- Incubation: The best way to incubate automation solutions is through short pilots. This allows you to start small and learn how to use RPA effectively before you move on to tackling more difficult business problems.

Stakeholders and Vocabulary

When you talk to people about RPA for the very first time, their expectation of what it can do varies widely. Sometimes what they think is closer to our definition of AI; at other times they won't believe that automation is at all possible. Your goal will be to navigate these expectations and provide the insight and vocabulary needed to understand the different types of automation available (chapter 1), the opportunities to which they are best suited (chapter 2), and the level of complexity involved to achieve each type of outcome.

Anyone who has over-inflated expectations of what's possible is likely to come up with complex scenarios to automate, the sort of task that's known to be difficult for employees to understand and complete. If you can't be clear about the process, you're going to find it hard to develop a solution.

You'd think that there would now be enough case studies to silence even the most vocal of your sceptics, but some may still need convincing. Engaging a partner who can provide a convincing demonstration of what RPA can achieve will help engage your stakeholders.

> If you're working with a partner at this stage, it can be useful to include a short demonstration to bring to life what RPA is capable of.

When people are faced with the prospect of automation, the first thing they think of are the scare-mongering "Robots are here to take your jobs" headlines they've seen splashed across the front pages of the Daily Mail. What then happens is that they become highly defensive as they think they need to protect their own positions.

Faced with this situation, explaining the five types of automation (chapter 1) will help your employees understand what RPA is all about, then you can start to talk about automation in a meaningful way and develop a common point of reference. Rather than concentrating on the negative, they'll be able to focus on the reality of RPA: the immediate win is an end to all the mundane, repetitive tasks that everyone hates, freeing them up for more interesting and challenging activities. These are the low-hanging fruit: the high volume, low complexity, potentially error prone tasks that are currently the bane of their lives.

The terminology used can be inconsistent, the industry itself is guilty of that, and this can lead to pedantic debates over what words or phrases mean. The first thing you need to do to engage stakeholders and help them understand the types of automation is to build a consistent set of terms, or common vocabulary.

Building a common vocabulary is a really effective way of debunking the myths and getting everybody talking in the same way. When I joined General Electric, all new starters were enrolled in a Six Sigma course; this gave us all a way to communicate consistently. So, it didn't matter who I was talking to, whether it was in aircraft engines or financial services, if I said "I've got a 3.8 Sigma process", they knew exactly what I meant because we all had that common vocabulary. When it comes to automation, giving everybody that common understanding means you can communicate with each other from the same point without any misconceptions

The breadth of scenarios that robotic automation covers can be overwhelming at first; classifying automation can help you simplify and focus the initial conversations to where the most value can be created for your organisation.

Where to Begin

At a major RPA and AI conference in London a few years ago, the participants were asked where their automation programmes had begun. Over 50% of respondents said that they started in their finance and accounting function. This was a common response at the time; finance functions are well-known for having mundane and repetitive elements to their processes, whether billing or journaling, they are high volume transactions that can be easily explained. Finance is also quite fortunate because they also have data already in electronic form; the people carrying out these processes are themselves being treated like robots!

F&A functions are still prime candidates for automation. The reason this was a popular starting point was because the majority of early adopters were banks. The high volume of transactions in their finance functions made them stand out as the areas where most time and effort were spent on repetitive tasks.

These days, the starting point is more balanced between finance and back-office operations. Both areas have the same level of repetitive task-based processes and both are looking for ways to grow, reduce cost, improve quality and deliver higher levels of customer satisfaction.

Every organisation is different but each one will have low hanging fruit that can be identified easily. Look for the business areas that carry out the highest volume of processes (usually where most people are located) and which areas have the highest amount of repetitive task-based processes (these are often the areas that have a higher number of junior employees, but this isn't always the case).

Building your Team

Back in chapter 3 I talked about business needs, the first of which was understanding the company motivation for beginning an automation programme. When you're building your first team, this motivation will have a significant influence on the approach you take and how you engage your team. Here are a few examples of how some organisations have started out on their automation journey:

- A business unit purchased the RPA software directly, started to use it and eventually expanded its usage more widely.
- The process improvement team implemented the RPA software and managed the ongoing changes as part of continuous improvement.
- An innovation team piloted RPA software successfully and supported its increased usage across the business.
- A support function collaborated with a consulting partner to demonstrate the opportunities of RPA through a proof of concept (POC) exercise.
- An IT department set up a project to implement RPA.
- A strategic project was started with immediate board support and funding available.

There's evidence that more RPA projects begin within a small area of the business and then widen their scope rather than begin as a strategic decision. If you find yourself in the rare position of implementing a strategic initiative, the decision to operate at scale has already been made - this will be covered in the next section. For most operations, it's best to start small, learn what automation can do, and build up your skills to take on more complex situations once you have the confidence from early successes.

Leadership

Even if you're starting your RPA journey small, there's something else to think about before you start. Organisations that were early adopters of RPA didn't have to worry about this, but now many employees have a real fear of automation because of negative articles in the press and as the threat of job losses increases.

I've heard stories of vendors being asked to talk to staff about RPA before the business has even really thought about the reasons for automation in the first place. This can put the vendor in an awkward situation if there is a backlash from employees who are afraid of the impending change. This is generally caused by over-enthusiasm and excitement for the project, rather than any negative intent.

Your first objectives are to think carefully about the reasons for beginning your RPA journey (Visual Game Plan in chapter 3) and to understand how you're going to communicate it to your employees. You'll need full senior management/board buy-in and clear leadership accountability to deliver the agreed objectives. More often than not, you'll find that the business is just carrying out a small trial (which doesn't raise employee concerns immediately) or is looking for growth, efficiency or quality improvements which should all be positive messages to convey to employees.

The person to lead your organisation's RPA programme is someone who's sufficiently robust to work in challenging environments and capable of operating as a maverick, but who can lead from the front at the most senior level.

Where organisations can fail most spectacularly is in identifying the right leadership for RPA programmes. If the person you choose to lead the programme doesn't have sufficient seniority, middle management can thwart your plans. If they don't have enough experience of transformation programmes, this can result in vendor led delivery. IT-led delivery can often lead to overweight processes and reduced ROI, while business-led initiatives run the risk of insufficient consideration of governance and structure which can lead to problems when you start to scale up. It's a minefield!

Recruitment agencies see this type of problem a lot. Businesses will often reject great candidates for the role, not because they didn't fit the role as defined but rather because they themselves don't have a clear idea of what types of resource they need.

One of the key leadership skills needed is to drive forward innovative technology and cultural change. Implementing RPA isn't just another technology project; it's a new way of working that will lead to new operating models. So, to summarise, the qualities of good RPA leadership are business transformation and change, innovation and process thinking.

Start Small

Piloting your automation project creates the framework that allows you to start small and learn as you grow. It reduces risk and tailors the programme to your business needs.

Experimentation

How easy it is to run short experiments to learn the capabilities of RPA will depend on the organisational culture. Do you have an existing culture of experimentation and innovation or is it a rigid command and control ethos? How engaged are your employees in the change process? The answers to these questions will give you an idea of the level of difficulty you'll face.

You'll *test and learn* many new ideas during the pioneering phase. If cultural change needs to be introduced, then starting small and showcasing results to the wider operation will increase the level of engagement needed for success.

One of the first opportunities for you to experiment may actually be in the way you evaluate multiple solutions. The criteria described in chapters 3 and 4 will help you narrow your shortlist down to a couple of vendors. The next step is to use both solutions to solve a small problem and evaluate how well they both perform. This will give you the insights you need to take forward into your first development and gain real experience in how easy or difficult the products are to use.

Leverage Existing Expertise

You may be surprised how many technically savvy people really take to the topic of automation (I'm referring to the majority of RPA solutions which are considered to be business-led as opposed to those which are more like a programming language). Good logical thinking and structured process design are great skills that aren't only found in people with a programming background.

You may also find that staff with a programming background are often frustrated by the simplicity of the RPA modelling environments and may prefer to return to their traditional programming roots.

Between these two extremes are business professionals who are tech-savvy or technical experts who are business-savvy: these are your ideal candidates for your RPA programme. And there are already many of them in your organisation, so your next challenge is to track them down!

Not all organisations have a rigid IT function, so whether ownership will sit in IT or in the business depends somewhat upon which solution you selected. Our main focus is on the tools that are classified as business technologies.

Leveraging existing skills within your own organisation is the solution to the challenge of limited resources available on the open market. Ideally you should still try to bring experience into the team through a direct hire or working with a partner who will help your employees learn. I'll look at the types of skills that you'll need in more detail in the next chapter.

Starting the Cultural Change

An engaged company culture will accelerate your plans for RPA adoption; a challenging culture will slow down or stop your plans entirely.

Case Study - Cultural Adoption

Five years ago, when I was working for a UK insurer, we set up an innovation function with the goal to accelerate the pace of change in the company. We started out looking at a range of new technical solutions that were generating a lot of market interest and we also started to think about the different ways of working that would be needed. The first two solutions we tested were low-code development and RPA.

Six months into our programme, it was clear that the

technology was robust and generally worked very well. It was the level of acceptance that now dictated whether the change would be adopted and that could make the difference between success and failure.

Eighteen months later, we found lots of people in the organisation saying they were planning to "test and learn" and then we knew we were beginning to make progress.

Selecting your first Process

One of the most frequently asked questions during conferences is: How do you choose your first process?

There isn't one simple answer, but there is an easy first pass you can take to highlight likely candidates. The first process has to be both a good fit for automation *and* have sufficient business impact to demonstrate clear value. Delivering the first solution is occasionally referred to as a proof of value; this is a useful description as value can refer to many different factors, which you can then use to showcase the wider potential of RPA across the entire business.

> A **Proof of Value** demonstrates that the solution works for your business

Look for the processes that take up the greatest amount of time. Multiplying the time taken to complete a single occurrence of the process by the volume of business transactions that are processed will give you the total time taken. This simple calculation will provide an initial view of the most time-consuming processes which will give you good initial candidates to evaluate further for potential automation opportunities.

When choosing your first process, look down your initial list and work out which IT systems are used most widely across the organisation. You don't want to begin with the most complicated scenario, for example, applications that have existing reliability issues, but at the same time you don't want to take the easy option of choosing IT systems that are only used by a small part of the company. You are looking for a typical process carried out by the business using core systems.

Another question you need to ask is completely non-technical and very subjective, and it's critical that you have a good understanding of your organisation's people and culture to answer it. Which of the business teams will have the strong sponsorship and leadership that you need to run an initial RPA pilot? Beginning your journey with a highly supportive area of the business is just as important as choosing the right vendor when you first start out. You're going to face people and culture challenges along the way and an engaged, empowered and supportive team will make your first steps that much easier.

Some organisations take weeks to decide on the first process to automate - this is more likely to be a defensive behaviour: someone putting obstacles in the way of progress. There's generally enough knowledge in the organisation to narrow your list down to a few suitable candidates for your pilot process without excessive analysis.

If you do need to do any further assessment, chapter 8 looks at a technique called the Process Prioritisation Funnel. It can be used during the pilot phase to help you choose the first process, but its real purpose is to help you assess and prioritise the *subsequent* processes.

Once you've narrowed your list down to the top 5-6 processes, you can make a judgement call on which ones are the best fit based on what you've learned about the types of automation possible; which processes are best suited to RPA; and which have the most manual operations.

Advantages of a Pilot Study

A pilot study, or pilot experiment, is a small-scale preliminary exercise carried out to evaluate feasibility, time, cost, adverse events, and improve upon an initial proposition before full scale implementation.

Starting small minimises any risk to the business, limits the scope to a small control group and helps you monitor performance closely. RPA programmes benefit from short iterative cycles of delivery that give a small amount of change between each revision. This further minimises risk while you're beginning to understand the skills needed to develop and deliver RPA. Regular updates to your bot also give you regular feedback so you can see that the solution is delivering the results you want.

Some of the key reasons to run an RPA pilot are that you can:

- Start small-scale so you minimise risk
- Learn the skills
- Evaluate impact, feasibility, time, costs
- Experiment with ideas, try variations
- Understand how it fits with people and the organisational culture
- Get customer/user feedback
- Identify risks or adverse events
- Predict the impact on the business when you scale up
- Make improvements to your solution and approach based on feedback from real examples

A pilot is different from the full implementation in several important ways: it involves just a few people rather than the whole team; the scope is often narrowed down to a single product or process rather than all the team's activities; and you can monitor performance much more closely as you have back-out plans that you can implement if there are any problems. To put it simply, a pilot limits the risk you take when you're first introducing RPA.

Operating a pilot will help you build confidence both in your own automation development skills and in gaining trust from stakeholders that the automated processes are operating reliably. Building this trust is a key objective as you begin your first development. The tool is still new so there needs to be enough flexibility in development to try different approaches and new ideas - in other words, experimenting with what's possible.

Finally, a pilot will allow you to fine-tune a solution that will operate in the real world. It's easy enough to create an automation script that meets your needs in the clinical conditions of a test environment, for example, populating fields in a Windows application with new data, but applications never run smoothly in the real world. Popup windows, help text, warning messages and other unexpected events all introduce new challenges that have to be overcome before the automation runs smoothly for every scenario and it can be scaled up to be used more widely within the company.

Even a small pilot will give you performance data about your new automated process. It allows you to explore the feasibility of the solution and measure the time, cost and quality impact you can expect to achieve at scale. It helps you identify challenges, risks and adverse events while still at a manageable size. Finally, it allows you to use that information to adapt your solution to meet the demands of running at scale, if necessary. You'll no doubt have an idea of how you expect the process to work, but reality can often be different. Running a small pilot gives you the chance to improve upon your initial model before you start operating at a scale that's wider and has greater impact.

If you still haven't narrowed your shortlist down to a single vendor, you should think about running multiple pilot studies, using the same process with each vendor. This will help you understand their differences in development time, implementation complexity and operational performance.

The greatest challenge with automation is usually not the technology itself but the culture you're implementing it in. I really can't over-emphasise the need to be very clear about how you're planning to communicate the programme and vision, and how you handle employee engagement: getting all this right is crucial in setting up for success.

Each organisation is different: different culture; different challenges; different levels of skill. Understanding all these factors will help you find the solution that's the right fit. This is not a "sheep-dip" kind of exercise where you simply follow what someone else is doing!

From a lean thinking perspective, it's fantastic to be able to get genuine customer feedback through small prototype iterations because the customer is the ultimate judge of what works. Even small-scale pilots can be very rewarding in the amount of feedback they provide from customers and users to improve the next iteration.

A pilot is rarely a one-and-done exercise; it's a cyclical approach where feedback from the previous cycle informs the changes and improvements you need in the next iteration. This is the BUILD-MEASURE-LEARN model defined by Eric Ries in The Lean Startup[43]. It gives you a framework to test new ideas, build solutions in a rapid iterative cycle, and get

---

[43] Eric Ries, 2011. The Lean Startup. Penguin Random House.

immediate feedback from users and customers. It works both in the pilot phase and later when you begin to scale up.

Measurement: Critical Success Factors

Critical success factors (CSF) - this is a management term that means *having the elements necessary for an organisation or a project to achieve its stated goal.*

There are a number of factors which will be critical to the success of your automation programme, the most common of which are described in the sections following. Throughout your programme you should monitor the CSFs to ensure you're on track and take corrective action if needed.

During the pilot phase, you'll need to start thinking carefully about CSFs for the first time. Describe clearly what the ideal state looks like for each one and what data you'll need to monitor the situation. There will also be other factors that you'll need to identify and measure in the context of your specific operation.

Executive Support

I've mentioned top-down executive support several times already as it's ideal to have this in place before beginning your automation journey. Historically however, automation programmes have not started with executive support and the starting points you find most regularly are:

- A small area of the business implements RPA before the wider organisation is aware. Many programmes have started this way, experimenting early and delivering rapid initial benefits. This approach eventually

leads to executive awareness and the opportunity for companywide adoption.
- Executive-sponsored activity (which can be a small scale POC or strategic programme) is becoming a more common starting point. Executive level engagement from the very start ensures a consistency of approach and message across the organisation and demonstrates commitment to the programme goals.

Target Operating Model

A Target Operating Model (TOM) simply describes how a business will operate at a point in the future. It is the Why (strategy), the How (processes and people), and the What (systems and capabilities) of your future operation.

You don't need to define a TOM at the beginning of the programme. What you learn from the pilot will help you evaluate the factors that will shape your future operation, how to scale up and what your new TOM will look like. Chapter 9 looks at the different operating models and how they might change as your RPA programme matures.

Conceptually, organisations will move through three phases of maturity, each of which may use a different operating model to nurture progress and advance most effectively:

- The pioneering phase encourages experimentation and new ideas, finding the way forward that's best for your organisation
- Scaling up means you'll have to introduce the governance and structure that will allow RPA to be implemented across the wider business

- Transformation occurs when you move into an operational mode of business; stability of ongoing operations and ongoing maintenance of your *digital workforce* will become the focus

Your TOM should provide a clear view of the target state for your organisational design: people (capabilities and behaviours), processes, and technology.

Leadership and Personal Drive

During the pioneering phase, your goal is to assemble a team that has the personal drive and enthusiasm to deliver your automation solution. Identifying the right leadership qualities to sail through new uncharted waters will be an important skill.

Leadership with the drive to push the programme forward, or better still, someone who's a little evangelical, will motivate others to sign up in the early phases when you're all still learning a lot yourself as an organisation and will ultimately help the programme to progress.

End User Education and Training

The early chapters of this book talked about how to educate your employees and stakeholders and give them the insight they need to make the journey smoother.

Educating and training everybody involved on the programme is a pre-requisite. It's too easy to focus entirely on the automation software as part of your skills development, but this is just one piece of a much larger jigsaw. The next chapter looks at how responsibilities are divided, but for now you'll also need to develop:

- Agile and collaborative working skills
- An in-depth knowledge of the business process that's being automated
- Business process improvement skills
- Automation testing
- Compliance / quality assurance

Agile and Collaborative Working

The Lean Startup mantra - BUILD-MEASURE-LEARN - is an example of an agile working approach, collaborating in a team to deliver the RPA solution in small increments.

Collaboration may be in the DNA of your operation or may be something that you need to work on. If it's something that needs to be developed then it will increase the level of difficulties you'll face when establishing the new ways of working best suited to RPA.

Strategy for Change

The actual implementation of the technology is usually not the greatest challenge you'll face; acceptance and adoption are more likely to be the greatest hurdles you'll have to overcome. These challenges will typically impact you from two fronts:

- The project team themselves may be working in a new and collaborative manner for the first time, using technology that's new to your company.

- The business areas may be fearful of change and the impact on their future career.

The pilot phase is when you build the foundations for continuous change. First you'll need to support both project team and business team with the necessary skills and knowledge for a successful implementation. Later, you'll need to provide ongoing coaching and mentoring support to help everyone understand the new ways of working.

Sustainable change requires behavioural change; you have to dedicate time and effort to move gradually towards the future state. This can be done in parallel with implementing your automation programme and, with each new implementation, the transition gets smoother.

Your governance processes need to reflect that you're in an early pioneering phase; you absolutely must avoid anarchy, but equally you should only add a control mechanism if its benefit to the programme is clearly understood and agreed.

Detailed Process

Chapter 7 looks at the applying lean thinking to benefit of your RPA programme. When you develop an automation script, you need a detailed understanding of exactly what users are doing and how the IT systems are behaving. Understanding both is essential for the development to begin. How the process works today is your first building block in creating the repository of information that you'll need to audit and change your processes in future.

There are conflicting opinions on whether you should optimise processes before, or after, automating. In the pilot phase, your main goals are to learn about RPA and its suitability for your business; at this stage, the argument about whether to optimise or not is less important. For now, here are some quick pros and cons:

- Optimising first will get rid of unnecessary activities - this may also include entire processes! This is particularly important when you have limited development skills, because it's wasteful spending time automating tasks that can or will be removed later.
- Optimisation, especially when conducted by a specialist core team, helps identify repetitive activities that can be developed into reusable modules. This in turn helps increase the speed of development and reduce the ongoing maintenance burden.
- Alternatively, if you automate first, you'll realise the benefits of automation more quickly and the automated process will give you extra data that will help you identify the opportunities for increased efficiency. Non-optimised processes are more complex so it's more difficult to change them later.

My personal preference is to optimise first but, whichever option you choose, you should also measure its benefits and impacts during the pilot phase.

Exception Management and Quality Control

The Customer Demand Model (also known as Runners, Repeaters and Rogues) will be explained in Chapter 8; this technique will help you identify tasks for automation (runners) and deal with the exceptions (rogues).

The real world is likely to be very different to your initial test environments, as there will be more exceptions to standard conditions than you anticipated. But that's ok; the whole purpose of running a pilot is to identify the differences and unexpected conditions before you implement fully.

Risk and Governance Sign Off (Steering Group)

When you set up your first pilot, you'll find that setting up a steering group of interested parties will help raise the education of these important stakeholders and will also give you the support you need to help the project succeed. The list below isn't exhaustive, but as a minimum these types of functional responsibilities (where they exist in your company) should be invited to be on the steering group:

- Business Executive
- IT / CIO / Security
- Risk and Compliance
- Audit
- Financial Crime
- Change Delivery
- Data Governance
- RPA CoE Lead (if applicable)

In smaller organisations, these may be functional responsibilities rather than separate roles.

The steering group isn't responsible for day-to-day operations; its remit is to ensure that adequate controls have been established to implement the changes in a structured way.

Robust End User Testing

End user testing is vital because it helps weed out problems early on. If an error happens during the pilot, the process can be stopped, so the impact is minimised. However, when the operation moves from pilot to scale, stopping processes can be severely disruptive. Robust end-user testing will provide a level of control and confidence for all stakeholders and users, even during the pilot phase.

One of the reasons that errors get through is because the person doing the actual automation development ends up taking on many of the key business roles, including testing. This is a BIG mistake. Firstly, if the number of developers available to you is limited the using them to perform testing makes that problem worse. Secondly it slows down the pace of change and, finally, the chances of errors getting through are much greater.

When you get to this stage, the quality of the testing will be one of your critical success factors.

Benefits Measurement and Tracking

What gets measured, gets done.

Before making *any* changes, you *must* first measure the current state of your operation. This may be a statement of the obvious, but you can't claim the automation is successful if you can't quantify how much improvement there's been. If you don't measure the starting point of your programme accurately before implementing change, you won't know the exact level of benefits achieved and could even risk the project being considered a failure.

Each of your critical success factors will likely have a measure (or number of measures) that will allow you to track whether or not you're successful in achieving your goals. When defining each of the critical success factors, it's also important to understand exactly what the definition is, what you're measuring, how you're measuring it, and what success looks like.

> Measure the performance of your business *before* implementing RPA so that you can accurately measure the impact.

Running and Evaluating a Pilot

Chapter 5 is the longest so far as it brings together everything you've learned in earlier chapters and gives you a structure to begin your RPA programme. Here's a checklist of your progress to date:

- Find a leader for your RPA programme
- Engage and educate stakeholders in RPA (create a common vocabulary)
- Set up a steering group
- Develop a vision and a game plan
- Set up the project team
- Choose a vendor based on business needs
- Provide training, coaching and mentoring for the team
- Communicate the goals and impact to employees
- Decide which process you'll automate first
- Measure the current state (pre-RPA)
- Optimise the process for RPA
- Set up an iterative development cycle:
    - BUILD: Develop and test the automation
    - MEASURE: Start small, pilot with just 1 person initially
    - LEARN: Refine your plans based on feedback
- Measure the impact (post-RPA)

Exercises

Make a list of key stakeholders in your own RPA programme. What are their roles?

- Make a list of potential processes for RPA (this will be further refined in chapter 8)

- What are your key measures of success? How will you measure this before implementing RPA?

- Who is in your pilot team?

Scaling Up

6. Six Key Responsibilities

If you search for jobs involving RPA on the Internet, you'll find there are hundreds of them. Even if you account for the creative use of synonyms in job titles, this still shows a high level of active interest in RPA.

RPA is also nothing particularly new; it's been around for over 10 years in its modern form. Most of the companies described in chapter 4 were formed in the early to mid-2000s, so there's been plenty of time to gain experience in RPA. Despite all this, between a third to a half of all new pilot projects fail[44].

Although the number one factor that slows progress is the shortage of skills[45], the learning curve for automation is relatively short compared to other development tools and approaches so the problem isn't complexity. Experience has shown that IT developers prefer to use traditional programming tools, as they think that the model-driven approach used by most RPA solutions is a dumbing-down of their technical skill-set. IT developers who have cross-trained into RPA have generally returned to using traditional programming languages because they see them as a greater intellectual challenge. This leaves a resource gap that needs to be filled, and it's this gap that gives new opportunities to people with business knowledge rather than technical programming skills.

---

[44] EY Report 2017 – Get Ready for the Robots http://www.ey.com/gl/en/industries/financial-services/insurance/ey-get-ready-for-robots

[45] Everest Group 2018 identified resource shortage as the Number 1 inhibitor to RPA growth https://www2.everestgrp.com/reportaction/EGR-2018-38-R-2691/Marketing

If you look at this from the perspective of the recruitment agencies, you'll see they have a very different view of the issue. The market is certainly buoyant at the moment, so a lot of them have teams that focus purely on recruitment into RPA and AI roles. The agencies have identified really challenging skills scenarios:

- Businesses don't know what skills they're recruiting for and reject good candidates.
- Businesses want to recruit candidates who have both RPA skills *and* the ability to implement standards, governance, process optimisation, project management, communication, cultural change and the roadmap (this list goes on!).

These two situations highlight the main problem: if you don't understand how to organise the wide range of skills you need to implement RPA, you'll expect applicants to cover an impossible scope of work and you'll end up rejecting good candidates that you should be hiring.

The size of your business is proportional to your specific needs. Small businesses will choose candidates with a range of skills while larger enterprises need scope for greater separation of roles and responsibilities. These considerations are the beginnings of Organisational Design for RPA.

Organisational Design is one of the key elements of your target operating model (TOM) and this is what I'm going to look at throughout the rest of this book. Right now, our focus is on roles and responsibilities.

When I talk about responsibilities in this chapter, I don't mean that each responsibility should be assigned to a different person on a one-to-one basis. You might be able to assign several different responsibilities to just one person within the project team because that person has the right skillset. In smaller organisations, and particularly during the pilot phase, it's more likely that some team members will take on multiple responsibilities.

Thinking about these responsibilities early will make it easier for you to scale up at a later stage, for example, adding dedicated resources to focus on specific areas that are showing the greatest degree of stress. Finding the right mix of different people to take on these responsibilities – as opposed to assigning everything to just one RPA developer - will help you get over the obstacle of limited technical RPA skills by using experienced employees within your operation that already have some of the knowledge you need.

This chapter on key responsibilities comes between the sections on Getting Started and Scaling-Up for good reason; the information in it has relevance to both topics. Understanding responsibilities will help you lay the foundations needed during the pilot phase at the same time as keeping an eye on the changes you'll need to make as you scale up.

If you've already been planning ahead and thinking about developing a centre of excellence, understanding which of these responsibilities will fit centrally and which belong locally is something that we will cover in detail in chapter 9.

1. Senior Leader

In pole position is your leader and RPA evangelist; this person is going to be the one who sets the vision for the programme, is influential at a senior level and generates the enthusiasm needed for an RPA programme to be accepted and adopted across the wider organisation.

Getting Started:

The RPA leader will have to have one eye on immediate needs and the other on the overall direction of travel. Their first responsibilities are to communicate with key stakeholders and bring the project team together.

In the beginning, the pilot team will need direction and leadership support to remove any barriers and engage the people you need to succeed. Although the structure will probably be quite fluid in the early stages, the goal will be to develop best practices that can be repeated as the programme scales up. So it's really important to think carefully about structure and governance.

In larger organisations responsibilities will include setting up and chairing the steering group to drive engagement and direction at the executive level while being accountable for ensuring appropriate standards are established and maintained.

One of the most crucial early leadership responsibilities is to come up with a clear communication plan that will address employees' concerns.

Scaling Up:

As the programme scales up, the leader will take a key role in raising awareness, celebrating success, showcasing the impact of early activities and sharing the lessons learned from early adopters as the number of people engaged in RPA increases.

One of the key elements of the leader's role is to continue evangelising the importance of RPA at a senior level. This is to ensure buy-in and support, as more time will now be needed to develop the strategy and vision for robotic automation.

At this point, the operational processes are in place, so now it's time to set up ongoing monitoring and performance reviews. Service Level Agreements (SLAs) must be created to define acceptable performance levels and to trigger a response when a problem occurs.

Scaling up means the team will need a new type of skillset. A key factor in moving from initial experiments to a robust operation is having people with the skills to set up clearly-defined repeatable processes for the programme.

Digital Transformation:

The transformation phase of an operation may need a different type of leadership style compared to the early phases. A pioneering and evangelical spirit is what's needed for Getting Started and Scaling Up, but industrialisation (or transformation) means that ongoing operations need to be stable and repeatable.

2. Business Process Improver

The Business Process Improver has the ability to solve problems, optimise processes through the elimination of wasteful activity and establish a culture of continuous improvement.

Getting Started:

The goal of the pilot phase is simply to get started and begin learning about RPA. You *will have to* implement governance and control processes; but you don't need to do this immediately. The best way to start is to keep your approach nimble and experimental, learning lessons as you progress. If you don't need to implement this kind of rigour during the pioneering phase, then don't!

If you already have these skills within your operation, you should be leveraging them from day 1; if you don't, you should begin to develop them pro-actively as they will be crucial to moving beyond the pilot phase.

One of the core skills of the business process improver is optimising processes; this is essential if your RPA programme is going to succeed. This skill might not be immediately available to you when you first start out; in this case, it's more important to get started and automate the *as is* situation, rather than delaying your kick-off. Don't hesitate to take advantage of these resources if they're available. If they're not available, don't delay, but start developing these skills as they'll be critical when you scale up.

Facilitation skills, which should be in any business process improver's toolkit, will be particularly helpful in workshops that educate and engage teams, and solve problems in a collaborative way.

> **Case Study: An Early RPA Adopter.**
>
> One of the early adopters of RPA was an Irish bank who didn't have a culture of continuous improvement or a team of business process improvers. When they were working on their first RPA process, they realised that if they didn't tackle the inefficiencies within their existing processes, it would mean:
>
> - Processes would be difficult to automate because there were wide degrees of variation in how different users carried out the same process, and this introduced a whole new level of unnecessary complexity
> - The opportunities that RPA could provide would not be fully realised
> - Maintaining the processes would be very difficult
>
> These findings were escalated to the RPA leadership team before the first automation was even complete. Recognising the problems early on gave them the opportunity to begin developing a solution and setting up a team of business process improvers to run alongside the RPA initiative.

Scaling Up:

When you operate at scale, you'll need to document and optimise your processes. A proven mechanism for deciding on the next process to automate is **the process prioritisation funnel**; this is covered in the next chapter. Your BPI team will give you the information you need: first they document the high-level knowledge, then they work on the detailed optimisation of the processes that have been identified as the next best automation opportunity.

Optimising processes for robots is different to optimising processes for people as many real-world constraints (available working hours, physical documents, availability of skills) are not applicable to robots. The ability to think in a logical manner and find the most efficient way to optimise the automated work differently to the original manual tasks will be an important skillset. The techniques typically used to document processes, such as standard operating procedures and flowcharts, translate well into all of the vendor solutions, giving you a clear template for each robot development.

As you move beyond your first couple of processes, you'll need to increase the rigour for process selection. This opens a window of opportunity to build up these skills, as shown in our case study. Documenting processes in a standardised and rigorous way also mitigates one of the key risks associated with automation: the loss of business knowledge.

An established BPI team will also educate and train the RPA development teams.

Digital Transformation:

Operating at scale is when the role of the business process improver comes into full effect. Where the software is more technical, the physical layer (systems of record) has to be separated from the business logic (processes); you need the technical experts to establish the foundations and the business logic to be built by process experts.

In agile organisations, the combination of both development and process skills happens naturally, often in a collaborative workshop format, and accelerates the pace of delivery even further.

More people have BPI skills than RPA skills; by separating these responsibilities, you create the opportunity to build more quickly. Business process improvers themselves often have enough technical ability to take on RPA development opportunities, and this is another way of leveraging existing skills to make up for resource shortages in key areas.

When operating at scale, optimising processes for automation becomes a key component of ongoing operational needs. It helps establish priorities, predicts the impact and shows everyone that efficient *automated* processes are very different to efficient *people-operated* processes.

3. Business Architect

The Business Architect's role is organisational design and developing the TOM. The evolution of operating models is covered in detail in chapter 9. A target operating model is the blueprint for how your future organisation will work.

Getting Started:

Many businesses do this naturally without really thinking about *how* they're going to do it or *where* the business is heading; there isn't any formal organisational design as the process is more organic and evolutionary.

The lessons you learned from the during the pilot phase are important as they show you what works well and what doesn't. All of this knowledge will inform you how to organise yourself at scale.

Strategic projects and large enterprises need more oversight and governance. Consequently they will only stay in the pioneering phase for a very short period before they have to implement the additional controls they need to scale up.

Scaling Up:

Business architecture defines three things: the current way your business operates; the future goal (the TOM); and the roadmap of how you move from one to the other.

The early experiments with RPA evolve naturally, generally without fixed ideas about what the future organisation will look like. Since activities are still small, this gives you the flexibility to adapt to the new situations you discover. This is why we call it a pioneering phase. When it comes to scaling up though, this will have to change from an evolutionary approach to one that's clearly defined and repeatable and that can be understood and applied by a greater number of people. When you look at the lessons learned from early experiments, you'll get an understanding of the impact automation has had and how your business model needs to change to implement RPA successfully at scale.

When the operation begins to scale up, it then becomes essential to measure, get feedback about and fine-tune the model. It's unlikely you'll get it completely right first time and you may have to adapt the model several times as the total number of people and functions involved expands.

You may believe that robotic operating models are completely new; this is not the case. You'll still need many of the same elements of traditional change management that you'll already be familiar with to ensure the changes are embedded so that the benefits can be realised.

Digital Transformation:

Implementing RPA is a paradigm shift that needs business transformation thinking, not simple evolutionary thinking. As the model shifts to a greater percentage of digital workers within your organisation, there will be a significant change in day-to-day processes. This will be explored in greater detail in chapter 9 (fine-tuning responsibilities).

Many of the processes for your *digital workforce* are the same as for your human workforce; compliance, regulation, retraining, and performance monitoring are all key components of your new robotic operating model.

4. Technical (or Enterprise) Architect

The technical/enterprise architect's role is to provide technology evaluation and guidance, operational configuration, maintenance and final solution design.

Getting Started:

Many RPA programmes begin without IT engagement. I'll look at the benefits of early IT involvement when I talk about operating models in chapter 9. One of the key factors to consider is the technology fit to evaluate your own business requirements for RPA successfully (chapter 4) and ensure that the solution works effectively with all existing IT systems within your entire technology infrastructure. For this the input of an IT technical architect is necessary.

In practical IT terms, the initial technology fit can be evaluated by running a Proof of Technology (POT) exercise. This is a short task that evaluates whether or not the vendor software can successfully function within your organisation's IT architecture and ensures that the software is compatible with your core systems. Vendor software capabilities vary greatly in their implementation and a POT will quickly reveal if there are any issues with installation and operation.

If you haven't chosen your RPA vendor by this stage, your goal will now be to do whatever's necessary to make that final selection.

Due diligence on the vendor themselves is also something that needs to be done when you start out. This is particularly the case for enterprise operations that have greater minimum standards of operation and governance. This will often have an impact on contractual arrangements later. Larger organisations will have existing security and safeguarding standards and obligations from third parties that need legal agreement. This all takes time, so it's worth starting early in parallel as soon as the pilot looks likely to be successful.

Before moving beyond the first pilot and beginning to implement your first automated process, the technical architect's responsibilities will be the final confirmation of the suitability of the chosen software and signing the contract.

Scaling Up:

Corporate overheads are – hopefully – less for small and medium sized organisations, but the same considerations apply. During the expansion phase you'll clearly establish that the solution you've chosen fits the business needs and this will help you avoid the risk of a proliferation of further RPA technologies.

Technical performance monitoring of both the RPA solution and the impact on underlying IT systems is a key technical element as the programme begins to scale up.

Digital Transformation:

An important ongoing element of solution architecture is a clear understanding of the wider technology stack. Changes will inevitably happen within the technology landscape and, as RPA reaches scale, it will become a mission critical component of the business operation. Clear communication of any changes to either system is necessary for them to integrate efficiently and to reduce the risk of failures because of unexpected changes.

I've established that accessing technical skills are one of the greatest challenges, so taking time to evaluate and select a single best-fit solution is the first step in maintaining skills in a single discipline. There may be good reasons for implementing multiple technologies, but you must evaluate all the risks and benefits before taking this approach.

The complexity of integration between applications will increase and the bots will become mission critical as the RPA programme scales up. Disaster recovery plans will need to be established and tested long before you reach this scale of operation.

5. RPA Developer

You may be asking why automation development and testing is so far down our list of responsibilities. In the first instance, it's because I've listed the responsibilities in a logical sequence of when they'll be needed. Development skills only become important when the software and first process have been chosen and you've set up your team.

It also emphasises the point I made at the beginning of this chapter; it's asking too much to hire an RPA developer thinking they can do everything to get your programme off the ground. In each phase of your evolution you'll need a flexible approach that can adapt to new findings and scale up when needed.

The responsibilities included with RPA delivery include automation development, testing, deployment and version control.

Getting Started:

The responsibility for automation development generally fits within the business. The next logical question is: Do business users have the skills to develop RPA or it should it be done by IT developers? There are three alternatives and your goal is to decide which of them fits your organisation best:

1. The software has been designed for technical users so programming skills are essential.
2. The software has been developed for users with either no or very limited technology skills; these tools have been designed for ease of use and can be developed by anyone, although programmers tend to dislike the limitations imposed.

3. The software isn't suitable for either highly technical programmers or general business people. Programmers find the software too basic and general business people have insufficient understanding of data, process and program construction. This technology is suited to suited to technically-savvy business users and business-savvy developers and is the most commonly used approach.

When you choose the software that meets your business needs, you avoid becoming embroiled in any debate and you select the one that's the best fit for your business model.

Don't overlook the matter of rigorous testing; the responsibility for this should sit with your pilot team to allow the development cycle to operate efficiently. When you're getting started, delivery tends to be slower and you'll come across unexpected (real world) problems. The automation developer is a terrific "Unit Tester" (testing the things that have just been developed) but often makes a poor user acceptance tester (who has to think about situations that could occur and have not been accounted for).

> ## Case Study – RPA Development
>
> When I put together my first automation team, they had previous experience of working as MI analysts within the business. They understood data manipulation and programming constructs, and were proficient in SQL (although this isn't generally needed for RPA) and VBA (Visual Basic for Applications). The fact that they understood both business processes and programming constructs made them ideal candidates to work on our first automation programme. In this case, the vendor developed our pilot automation with the team working alongside to learn from their experience.

Scaling Up:

Most significantly, scaling up involves increasing the overall size of the team. When the programme first starts out, team members may take on multiple responsibilities, working together to fill any gaps that might exist in the team. As the team grows, it's important to reassign specific roles to individuals, and specialisation in certain skills becomes increasingly likely. Specialisation is the assignment of a single responsibility to an individual or group. For example, the responsibility of user acceptance testing might have been shared between team members when first starting out but will now be given to a dedicated team member.

When you move beyond your first process, you'll have to develop more complex situations and test new concepts; sharing the lessons learned will inform your first-generation operating model.

New people joining the team will benefit from the experience of existing team members which supports their learning. A centre of excellence will begin to form naturally; as the team grows, the more experienced employees become mentors to the less experienced and take on responsibility for the more complex problems.

As the centre of excellence develops, a core team often becomes a specialist resource responsible for horizon scanning, training and providing shared resources to support local development teams.

Digital Transformation:

Testing also becomes mission critical when operating at scale. As well as testing new automation, the testing of changes to existing automation and regression testing (backwards compatibility of changes) will become an additional responsibility.

RPA software updates also need greater planning as a significant amount of testing is necessary when a major upgrade is released. Software advances must be understood and communicated to the wider team.

When you reach a truly industrialised phase where the majority of processes suitable for RPA have been automated, there will be another shift in the operating model, moving responsibilities into a centralised team.

6. Operations Support

Once you reach scale, a new role will be needed to take on responsibility for ongoing maintenance of existing robotic automations, monitoring, re-training and optimising robot use across the portfolio. Small businesses may never reach a point where this role is necessary; large enterprises may find themselves considering this as early as the completion of their first process.

An operations function will maintain existing robotic automations. They must be available 24/7 to ensure that the bots are performing correctly and any problems are handled immediately.

Getting Started:

There won't normally be any operational responsibilities during the pilot phase; this develops as you scale up. The first few processes are usually managed by the pilot team themselves.

Scaling Up:

Before setting up a full-time operations function, you need to think about organisational size as this has a big impact on the number and size of processes you're going to automate. Operations will be responsible for monitoring your *digital workforce*, correcting problems and escalating critical issues.

The existing organisational design may also influence your decision at this stage. Companies that already have operations functions will tend to make use of these capabilities rather than setting up something new.

Digital Transformation:

Small and medium sized companies generally look for partners that can handle operational needs rather than developing the capability themselves. These partnerships often come with the added benefits of providing additional capacity on-demand to meet surges of activity, even if the software provider doesn't offer this option as part of their standard contract. If businesses are used to operating 9-5 only, introducing out of hours operations can be difficult in which case, working with a partner is a good option to consider.

Larger enterprises are usually in a better position to handle 24/7 operational support and maintenance needs because they already have them in place for their core systems.

Exercises

List the six responsibilities on a page, add the members of your team and specify who will take each of them. Remember that individuals may take on multiple responsibilities in the pilot team.

7. Applying Lean Thinking to RPA

Lean is a business methodology focused on customer value, empowered people and waste elimination. The reason I've included it is to highlight the benefits of lean principles, tools and techniques that will improve and accelerate the delivery of RPA.

Automation has been one of the elements of lean thinking even before the approach was known as Lean. Automation provides new ways to increase quality, eliminate errors, reduce the time taken to carry out a process and increase customer satisfaction. Modern RPA is simply the latest technological advance that is being incorporated into the Lean practitioner's toolkit.

Lean was originally a manufacturing methodology created by Toyota in the 1950s. Applying automation to the business goes all the way back to the founder of Toyota, Sakichi Toyoda, who used the term "Auton-omation" to describe the goal of introducing automation with human intelligence.

Toyota recognised that there was a need for human intelligence when the machinery carried on working even though a problem had occurred. The simple solution to this was *Stop on Defect:* if a problem was detected, the machine would stop immediately and wait for human intervention.

Lean is a learning approach; it adapts continually, including new tools and techniques whenever they are discovered. Books such as the Lean StartUp have shown us how Lean has moved from its roots in car manufacturing to developing innovation in a world of start-ups.

Lean thinking has also continued to evolve as a business philosophy. Many global companies have now adopted Lean principles. The application of Lean in business or in manufacturing describes a philosophy that applies a collection of tools and techniques into business processes to optimise time, resources, assets, and productivity while improving the quality level of the products or the services delivered to customers.

Creating efficient (do things right) and effective (do the right things) processes has always been at the heart of the Lean approach. But it's much more than just about process, it also provides the techniques to aid building, deploying and operationalising strategy. Lean transformation is a term used to describe the deployment of Lean thinking across an entire organisation.

Toyota worked closely with their partners to establish a win-win situation for all involved, recognising the different skills needed and collaborating to achieve the best result; this model can most likely be applied to your own RPA programme as well.

The concept of continuous flow is central to Lean thinking; it describes the situation where you move from step to step in any given process as quickly and efficiently as possible with minimum delay (maximum value-add, minimum waste). Lean practitioners are always looking to find new ways to automate tasks, and RPA is now part of the solution.

Getting Started with Lean RPA

> 🔑 People often focus on the robot in RPA, don't forget about the **process**

Many organisations focus on the technological advances that enable us to imitate human interactions but forget to look at the processes in any depth, because they assume that what we do today is good enough. Doing this leads to automation that's difficult to develop, prone to failure and time-consuming to maintain. Lean gives us the tools and techniques to define, optimise and deliver efficient, flexible and easy to maintain automations.

The methodology used in the book The Lean Startup is a great fit for RPA programmes: cross-functional teams collaborate on each new iteration of the automated process, developing, testing and measuring the impact on the customer. When applied to RPA, this approach will help you to understand how automation can best support your organisation and your customers.

These techniques work particularly well because of the interactive nature of many of the development tools which make it easy to quickly try different ideas and get immediate feedback on the result. However, different tools require different types of skills, so the right way to do it is to find the right solution for your organisation, rather than trying to make your organisation fit the solution.

Lean is frequently used to describe the function of continuous process improvement within an organisation. Lean principles, tools and techniques provide the foundations of good process design before automation begins, by eliminating unnecessary work and optimising the remaining tasks.

One of the concerns frequently raised by increasing levels of automation is that the business risk of losing process knowledge and technical expertise, as the number of robots increase and people with that knowledge move into new roles. Applying Lean thinking techniques will help you understand, standardise and fully document your processes before automation begins, then you'll find that many of these risks are reduced and that the knowledge is retained within the organisation.

Another key benefit of automation is improving the quality of the end result. The starting point for many lean processes is to have *Quality-Built-In*, in other words, to design a solution that is right first time, every time. My first exposure to automation involved a process which duplicated data across multiple IT systems. There was a high volume of data and this occasionally resulted in errors being made. Correcting them often took a lot of time as they were never discovered quickly and you would need changes across all the systems to resolve. The redesigned automated process changed the sequence of steps to validate the initial input data against a reliable data source. Once this was done, the accuracy of the data in all underlying IT systems was 100% guaranteed. With *Quality-Built-In*, rework and painful duplication was eliminated.

Scaling Up with Lean RPA

Scaling-up means moving beyond the pilot. When we reach this phase, Lean thinking can again help us by giving us techniques such as Lean strategy deployment, good organisational design and clear operating models to deliver an automation strategy.

Just-In-Time (JIT) is a concept of lean thinking that made its way into general business usage long before it was more widely recognised as part of Lean. JIT is a concept that means you have exactly the materials you need at the point you need them. In the manufacturing sector, this often will be a piece of real equipment; JIT means that it's delivered just ahead of when you need it, rather than the old way of tying up capital by holding inventory in huge warehouses.

The same is true for many business services which need information (rather than inventory) in real-time. This is easier said than done when the information needed is spread across multiple IT systems, all of which need to be accessed to complete the process. The clearest example of this is when a call centre agent responds to a customer query, they are skilled at keeping the customer talking while in the background they are frantically navigating through multiple IT systems and menus to retrieve the information they need.

Automation can significantly help the call centre agent, giving them the information they need in real time (or *Just In Time*). Once the information needed to identify the customer or policy has been taken the automation immediately retrieves the necessary data from different applications and presents it back to the call centre agent much more quickly than the agent could have achieved manually. The agent has the information exactly when they need it: *Just-In-Time*. Sometimes RPA is described as taking the robot out of the human: it does the mundane tasks which frees the person up to focus on the value add, providing the service the customer wants.

Your organisation will need to have a continuous improvement culture to sustain your RPA programme and ensure that you find opportunities for further advances as your RPA programme matures.

Customer – People – Process

When you begin your RPA programme, you may be tempted to automate the identical processes you do today; the *As Is* situation. The danger in doing this is that you may not be implementing the most efficient process and therefore miss opportunities for improvement. In the worst-case scenario, these processes no longer meet customer requirements and aren't needed anymore. Applying Lean thinking will give you solutions that meet customer needs through efficient processes and develop a company culture that's supportive of change. A nice and easy way to introduce Lean concepts is to get your team to think about Customer, People and Process:

Customer

What is Value from a Customer Perspective?

Lean thinking is a customer-centric approach; your goal should always be to understand the steps that add value *from the customer's point of view*. When you're collaborating with a team internally, put yourself into the customer's shoes and ask: Does this add value? If you're not sure, you'll need to test your thinking by talking directly to customers to get the immediate feedback you need.

Customer demands are constantly changing; the introduction of RPA provides the tools to deliver on their needs even when the underlying IT systems don't.

People

Empowered, engaged, enthusiastic people are at the very heart of Lean thinking principles.

You need an empowered team that will take ownership and accountability for what needs to be done. Providing them with the right skills to do the job and solve any problems helps them achieve this goal.

Process

A process is a series of steps or tasks that when all completed achieve an outcome. When you begin evaluating your processes, you need to scrutinise each task to see if it adds value to your customer outcome or not. Anything that does not meet this criterion should be removed or revised and the remaining activities be rearranged into their most efficient order. When you look back at a revised process, you check against these measures to evaluate if it has been fully optimised:

- Efficient - Zero waste
- Capable - Delivers what is needed when it is needed
- Flexible – Adapt easily to changing circumstances

Customer Demand: Runners, Repeaters, Rogues

Having created a common vocabulary for your stakeholders, the next step on your automation journey is to think about your customer, and most importantly, customer demand. This concept is one of the most critical building blocks in your lean foundations so I'm going to look at this first from a lean perspective and then see how it can be applied directly to the needs of your RPA programme.

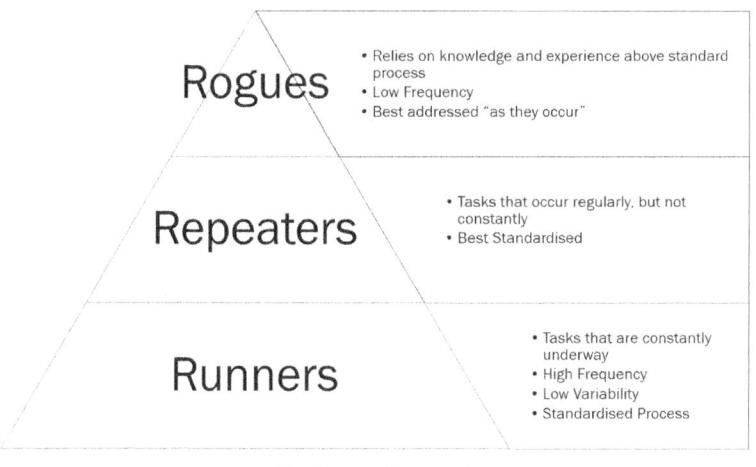

Rogues
- Relies on knowledge and experience above standard process
- Low Frequency
- Best addressed "as they occur"

Repeaters
- Tasks that occur regularly, but not constantly
- Best Standardised

Runners
- Tasks that are constantly underway
- High Frequency
- Low Variability
- Standardised Process

Customer Demand

The technique is called the 3 Rs.

- Runners: these are the most frequent tasks carried out by an organisation, usually driven by the high levels of customer demand. They account for the greatest level effort expended and, due to the volume, or typically serviced by a dedicated team.

- Repeaters: these occur less often and have periodic demand. The way these processes are handled can vary widely from organisation to organisation.
- Rogues: these are sometimes referred to as strangers. They have sporadic or infrequent demand, or are exceptional occurrences and are usually handled by technical experts.

Runners

Runners are high-frequency, low-variability tasks; they're very standardised and are usually given to teams that simply follow the steps in a process. These processes require relatively little subject knowledge or judgment. Many large organizations find up to 80% of their effort is spent on runner tasks.

Repeaters

Repeaters occur less frequently, for example, month- or year-end processes, or ones that are driven by seasonal variations, for example, the tax year-end.

They are a challenge for organisations that try to smooth out peaks of activity so they have a more consistent level of demand over time (a process called levelling). Sometimes that's simply not possible and organisations have to find ways to service peak demand. To do this, they may hire temps or employ more staff than is necessary at other times of the year, but, in this scenario, avoiding a decline in customer satisfaction means incurring higher costs.

Rogues

Rogues are usually handled by your technical experts. Compared to runners, they are low-frequency occurrences and are only addressed *as* they occur. They generally rely on expert knowledge and experience to complete.

> ### Supermarket Sweep
>
> A good way of describing the difference between runners, repeaters and rogues is to imagine a supermarket checkout. You've put all your goods on the conveyor belt, then the checkout operator takes each item and passes it across the scanner into the packing area. The checkout operator is a runner: they are following the standard process of scanning each of your items.
>
> Suddenly one of the items won't scan, the checkout operator doesn't stop what they're doing and leave the checkout to find a replacement. Instead they put the item to one side and turn on the light that alerts the supervisor, then they continue scanning the remaining items. The supervisor knows the store layout and their job is to find a replacement. In the meantime, the checkout operator carries on scanning the rest of your items, keeping the runner process going. The supervisor comes back with the replacement item which can then be scanned.
>
> In this analogy, the item that won't scan is the defect, the process error; the supervisor is the equivalent of the technical experts in your business processes, using their knowledge and skill to deal with rogues.

> When you're at the checkout, you notice it's busy and queues are building up. Over the tannoy, you hear the announcement that all multi-skilled employees should go immediately to the checkouts. This is your repeater scenario: some employees have been cross-trained on checkout operations so they can service periods of peak demand. Additional checkouts will open and the queues soon reduce.
>
> This is an analogy for a typical business process. In the supermarket, you don't want the checkout operator suddenly heading off to look for a replacement item; in the business, you don't want someone without technical expertise wasting time trying to solve a problem they are unequipped to resolve. Conversely, you don't want your technical experts going through very simple task-based processes. You always want to organise yourself so you make the most efficient use of available resources. At periods of peak demand businesses have surge plans, similar to the multi-skilled employees who can be diverted to operate the checkout in periods of high demand.

Applying 3Rs to RPA

Don't look for a 100% solution to every process, the 80/20 rule (known as the Pareto principle) will apply: focus on the 80% of the process that only requires 20% of the effort! If you follow this thinking, you'll avoid wasting time trying to automate the last 20% which takes 80% of the effort!

The 3Rs model can also be used to articulate how different automation solutions can be used to process business in your own organisation. Here's how the 3R's can be applied to RPA:

- Runners are a great starting point for RPA; the activities are very high-volume, task-based and rote. These are your low-hanging fruit. Runners give you your first candidate processes; whether they will be attended or unattended doesn't really matter, that will be a choice once you drill down into the actual processes themselves. Runners get you started and are the sweet spot for RPA.
- Repeaters are less frequent so they're difficult to resource for reasons I've described previously. Automation gives you an option you've never had before: the ability to scale up or down very easily to match seasonal or peak demands without having to hire temps or hold on to extra employees. Vendor licensing models vary so this is not a universally available option. If it isn't directly available from your vendor, third party suppliers can also provide this option as a value-added service.
- Rogues are outside the capability of attended or unattended RPA but can be suited to chatbots or cognitive and machine-learning solutions. Not too long ago we would have said this is outside of the scope of RPA entirely and something that would only be possible by knowledgeable employees. Machine Learning is changing this view as it becomes possible to automate some elements of human thinking.

Runners, repeaters and rogues are a high-level view of processes: one that which senior management and stakeholders can easily understand. Identifying which processes are runners, repeaters and rogues helps you choose the right solution to fit your needs. A runner process absolutely has to be the starting point for your next RPA implementation. The next chapter looks at how you prioritise processes for automation in greater detail.

Optimising Processes using Lean Thinking

A technique for optimising and improving processes taken from lean thinking is the *seven types of waste*. The seven types of waste help your team to challenge each step of the process and make changes that will eliminate wasteful activities. The seven types of waste are broadly broken down into three categories: People, Quantity, and Quality:

People Waste

1. Over-processing: doing unnecessary and non-value adding tasks.
2. Waiting: inactivity during the process, increasing the customer wait time.
3. Motion: excessive movements to get everything needed together to complete a piece of work.

Quantity Waste

1. Inventory: holding too much stock or having too much work in progress (for example, a claim, an incident, a sale can all be classified as inventory in your process).
2. Transport: the movement of items from one place to another.
3. Overproduction: producing and storing an item before it's needed.

Quality Waste

1. Defects and excessive inspection: defects are problems that prevent the process from operating smoothly; excessive inspection is over-checking an item to ensure it's up to standard.

There's a useful mnemonic that can help you to remember the seven types of waste. If you rearrange the first letter of each type of waste, it spells out the name TIM WOOD (Transport, Inventory Motion, and Waiting, Over-processing, Overproduction, Defects).

How often do you spend time searching for information? This could be in policy documents, FAQs or on a website knowledge base; this is an example of *motion* waste. The act of using the information adds value; spending time trying to find it in the first place is wasteful.

Chatbots can eliminate waste from a process as they allow for natural language understanding (whether written or spoken) to provide immediate results to user queries. Static information such as procedures, standardised documents or frequently asked questions are spread across multiple locations within your organisation, which is why they take time to find when needed. Simple chatbots can be used to navigate quickly to the information you need, eliminating the wasted time searching through all the different sources, and delivering the information you need.

As a business methodology, Lean gives you the framework that will help you realise the full potential of RPA.

Exercises

- Look at your own processes and think about the customer demand model. Identify examples of Runners, Repeaters and Rogues.

- Process optimisation: choose a core business process you're familiar with and see if you can find examples of each of the seven types of waste in it.

8. Prioritising Processes for Continuous Delivery

The Process Prioritisation Funnel

- All Processes
- Divisional or Functional Priority
- Time * Volume
- Prioritisation Criteria
- Select
- Automate

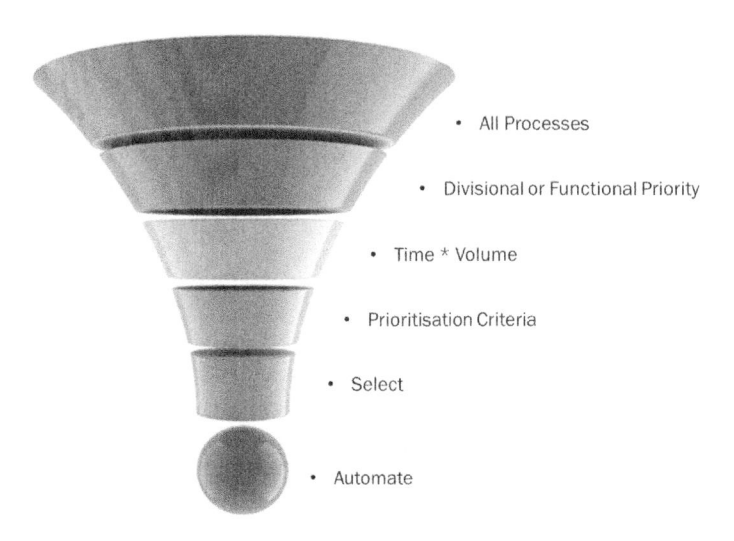

Process Prioritisation Funnel

The process prioritisation funnel is a technique that helps you quickly narrow down which process to automate next. It can be applied during the pilot phase to help you choose the first process, but its real benefit is in establishing an ongoing procedure for prioritising the processes to be considered for automation.

Ongoing prioritisation might seem like an enormous task; it's easy to understand why some organisations fall into a sudden state of analysis paralysis at this point as they try to evaluate the impact of RPA on every process. The process prioritisation funnel helps give you a reasonably accurate view on which process you should automate next to deliver the greatest benefit. The alternative is to evaluate every process in advance, but this has many downsides because it takes time and a lot of effort. What you get with the process prioritisation funnel is a trade-off: it won't give you the perfect information for every scenario but it will make bold assumptions to help you find the process that's most likely the next best one to automate.

Level 1: Identify Every Process

The first level looks like a simple starting point. But it isn't.

It's very rare to find a list of all the processes used within your organisation. If you can, fantastic! At this level, organisations who have implemented workflow management or BPM are ahead of the game; they probably will have a comprehensive list of processes and good data to know how much time and effort is being used to service each one of them. They can move directly to level 2!

For everyone else, there's some good news and some bad news. The *bad* news is that you're going to have to get all this information together. The *good* news is that you don't need all of it immediately! Knowledge of the business and a few simple rules will help you focus on the most likely candidate areas and identify your first process, avoiding analysis paralysis and getting started quickly.

Focussing on the wrong areas first really isn't a big deal; you'll always be working on the most important processes based on the information you have available at the time. The process prioritisation funnel is a self-correcting model: as more information becomes available on new processes, the ones with the greatest impact will rise to the top of your priority list.

Your goal will be to get all this information together, but as it happens in parallel with the other activities, it should be done with a degree of priority order. The information you need at level one is:

- Process Name
- Process Purpose/Goal
- Process Owner
- Functional Area (Function/Department/Division/Team)
- Estimated Transaction Volume (Annual and notable Peaks of Processing)
- Estimated Touch Time (Employee effort expended in the completion of an average case)
- Approximate Total Effort (Volume * Touch Time)
- Customer Facing / Back Office [Optional]
- Process Classification [Optional, see Runners/Repeaters/Rogues]

The processes that fit into the runner category are typically the ones you're looking for when you start to try and identify the next best process to automate.

Output to Level 2: Priority based on identification of runner processes and estimated effort.

Level 2: Functional Priorities

Functional priorities fall into two primary types:

- Business areas that have been identified as a strategic priority for operational growth
- Business areas that are off-limits due to other in-flight activities (a system change for example)

Strategic priorities are an important factor for RPA. When developing your strategy and game plan for RPA (Chapter 2), any existing functional priorities should have been identified and recorded in the targets section. Examples of strategic priorities you may encounter are:

- If your strategic goal is to reduce back-office costs, your initial evaluation should focus on back-office functions. The first step of functional evaluation will be to identify the costs attributed to processes in these areas and show you which are the biggest opportunities for the next level of prioritisation.
- If your strategic goal is to increase sales of a specific product, your initial evaluation should focus on all the processes that support that product and work out which of them will have the greatest impact on sales. Customer feedback will be a key factor in your evaluation.
- If the strategic goal of a pensions business team is to improve the customer journey, they should first focus on the end-to-end pensions process. A full lean thinking evaluation to optimise for automation will identify the processes that will deliver impact most quickly.
- A specific business area has a backlog that generates complaints and rework. RPA can be used in several ways to help to begin the backlog recovery. It can provide *tactical* (short-term) solutions which are used to resolve the backlog situation only and *strategic* solutions that can improve the problem process in the future.

If there are specific areas of your business that are temporarily off limits, you can leave them out of your initial level 1 evaluation. This will allow you to move more quickly into those functions where employees and opportunities are available, for example:

- A new claims system is being implemented and the business team is already fully engaged in carrying out the testing and training that's needed before the new system is rolled out. If the existing claims system is about to be replaced, there's unlikely to be much benefit in automating due to the short time available.
- A finance team working on time-critical year-end processes may put them temporarily out of scope until the work has been completed.

Level 2 is a pragmatic approach to taking a simple first cut of available processes for prioritisation. Even though some areas may be marked as currently off-limits, it's still worth checking to see if RPA provides a better alternative to the one currently being applied.

Output to Level 3: Priority based on good fit business functions containing runner processes, and high estimated effort

Level 3: Highest Total Effort (Time and Volume)

Level 3 begins with a detailed data collection of time and volume that will give an accurate view of total effort. This information may be available in MI or BPM systems, if not, you'll need to carry out a manual data collection exercise.

Processing volume information is often readily available through typical SLA reporting; the touch time (the average amount of time taken to complete a case) is generally less readily available and so you'll need to put together a data collection plan.

In addition to the data collected in stages 1 and 2, you now need:

- Transaction Volume (Annual and notable Peaks of Processing)
- Touch Time (Employee effort expended in the completion of an average case)
- Total Effort (Volume x Touch Time)

Automating the processes with the highest total effort is most likely to give you the greatest benefit; this evaluation is not comprehensive but it will quickly give you a prioritised list of processes which can go on to the next level for further assessment. Level 3 gives you the first set of priorities for automation.

Output to Level 4: Priority based on good fit business functions with highest total effort

Level 4: Prioritisation Criteria

The previous step has given you a rough prioritisation; now you need to begin documenting the process in greater detail. You'll need to apply additional evaluation criteria that will increase the level of confidence in which processes provide the greatest benefit, as they can come in many shapes and sizes.

A SIPOC (Supplier-Input-Process-Output-Customer) gives you the opportunity to take a high-level view of the process in question and now provide a rough evaluation. The next section looks at the types of criteria used for evaluation in more detail: these include:

- Return on investment (ROI)
- Level of manual activity
- Operational impact
- Rule-based activities
- Number of defects
- Re-use

How these factors are weighted will vary by business; the collective best-fit of these criteria will help you prioritise those processes that have the highest level of impact with low to medium levels of complexity.

Output to Level 5: Priority based on weighted scoring of prioritisation criteria

Level 5: Select

Before you begin working on process optimisation and automation, the final selection criterion is to do a full evaluation of the suitability of the area in which the automation will be developed. This means evaluating the suitability of leadership, availability of people and the environment in which the team will be working. Any of these may be challenges but, with some thought and preparation, you should be able to deal with them before starting automation

Ironically, the final stage of the process prioritisation funnel requires human evaluation of the circumstances to deliver the final prioritisation!

Output to Level 6: Priority based on weighted scoring of prioritisation criteria and readiness of area to begin automation

Level 6: Automate!

When process automation development begins, the priority of the selected process is locked. As new information on other processes becomes available, the priorities will change, so when it's time for each new process to be developed, the item selected is based on the priority information available at the time.

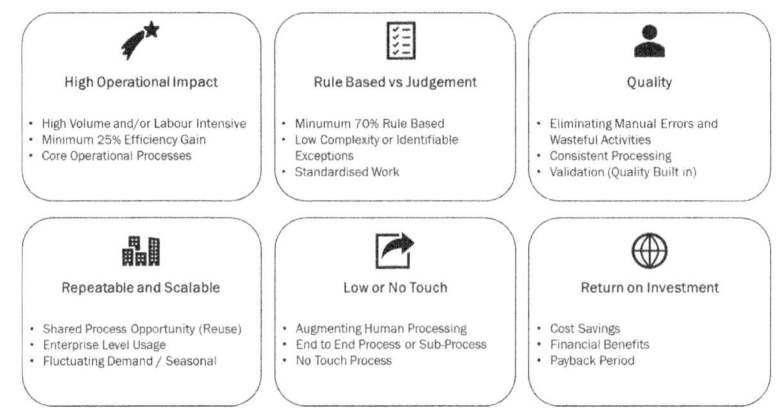

Process Prioritisation Criteria

High Operational Impact
- High Volume and/or Labour Intensive
- Minimum 25% Efficiency Gain
- Core Operational Processes

Rule Based vs Judgement
- Minumum 70% Rule Based
- Low Complexity or Identifiable Exceptions
- Standardised Work

Quality
- Eliminating Manual Errors and Wasteful Activities
- Consistent Processing
- Validation (Quality Built in)

Repeatable and Scalable
- Shared Process Opportunity (Reuse)
- Enterprise Level Usage
- Fluctuating Demand / Seasonal

Low or No Touch
- Augmenting Human Processing
- End to End Process or Sub-Process
- No Touch Process

Return on Investment
- Cost Savings
- Financial Benefits
- Payback Period

Process Prioritisation Criteria

Level 4 of the process prioritisation funnel gives you the opportunity to define and weigh a set of criteria that works for your business. I've listed 7 common criteria below and you should think about adding your own if appropriate.

Criteria 1 - High Operational Impact

Level 3 of the process prioritisation funnel (the highest total effort) is a simplified, and therefore imperfect in itself, way of identifying the highest operational impact. When you've narrowed down the number of processes that need to be assessed, you can spend the time to drill deeper and apply a more refined definition.

Operational impact applies to all operational factors; depending on the type of process this could include cost, productivity, throughput, level of waste, rework, wait time, efficiency, etc. In your evaluation you'll be looking for processes that will return a minimum of 25% efficiency improvements if automation is applied.

Criteria 2 – Rule Based vs Judgement

Runner processes are task-based and can be clearly explained and understood even if you're new to the job; there's very little need for knowledge or judgement. Junior staff usually start off on these rule-based processes because they will have little or no experience.

If the decision-making rules can be clearly explained then they can be easily implemented through automation. However, if the decision needs to be based on experience and knowledge, this isn't a good initial candidate for RPA.

If 70% or more of the process is rule-based, it's a high priority candidate for automation. It will be a low complexity process and/or have a low number of identifiable exceptions. If you have an established BPI team, these processes should have already been standardised and the work instructions that explain the process steps already in place.

Criteria 3 – Quality

The Six Sigma methodology measures process capability. It's a measure of how often the process runs perfectly; when it doesn't run perfectly, it's called a defect. Introducing automation will improve process quality and eliminate any defects.

When a process generates an error, it creates extra work. This is called failure demand: unnecessary rework correcting manual errors that has to be done after the process has finished.

Your goal in automating the process is to get rid of those manual errors and wasteful activities. Validation is a central part of the process, removing any errors and making it as straight through processing as possible.

Criteria 4 – Repeatable and Scalable

It's important to think about the impact of repeater processes (chapter 7) and evaluate them as candidates for automation. This gives you a great opportunity to level out the resource demands for the process. The goal here is to provide a solution to the staffing problems that you get during seasonal peaks.

Some RPA tools benefit hugely from the development of reusable standard components. A very cost-effective way to begin is to develop a few components that can be re-used later in other processes. Clearly, this will need extra preparation and development time in advance but the result is time saved longer term.

In Chapter 9 I'll talk about industrialising your RPA programme. One of the advantages of a centralised RPA development team is that they are in a great position to identify common processes across multiple business areas.

Criteria 5 – Low or No Touch

Look for processes that need very little user interaction; they are good candidates either for automation of the entire processes or for smaller steps in an overall process. If no interaction is needed at all, it could be a candidate for unattended processing; steps that do need interaction will be better suited to attended automation.

Criteria 6 – Return on Investment

The payback period is the amount of time it takes to recoup the costs of implementing automation from savings or growth. This is effectively the break-even point for your project. The costs are a combination of licensing, development time for all employees involved in the project, and any ongoing maintenance costs.

ROI is expressed as a percentage and has to be calculated over an explicit timeframe. The formula is *benefits attained* divided by *costs*. Both costs and benefits can be difficult to measure and track, so spending time to work out what you need and how you're going to get the required data will be an important step.

- If you're in a growth scenario, the benefits can be calculated as cost avoidance (you avoid the need to recruit additional employees at the typical rate).
- If you move employees to other roles or functions, the associated reduction in costs won't occur until the person moves. The move may also incur additional costs, such as training, which will reduce your immediate benefits.

In the same way that there will be ongoing operational costs, the benefits are perpetual, so it's quite reasonable to calculate a 1-3-year ROI. Organisations that are looking for more immediate impact may measure ROI over a shorter timescale.

Criteria 7 – Innovation

The goal of many businesses is to deliver innovative new products and services. Although RPA is generally considered a solution for integrating applications and automating existing processes, many capabilities of its tools can be applied to the challenge of innovation, developing entirely new processes to test innovative new ideas.

The first 6 criteria all look at existing processes; this final one should encourage you to look for opportunities to create processes that don't currently exist:

- RPA can deliver a new interface that sits above existing IT systems. The new interface can be used to change the process sequence and evaluate the effectiveness of new working practices.
- RPA can make adjustments to the existing Windows interface, by manipulating the information displayed or even triggering completely new activities as the application is used in its typical manner.
- Many RPA solutions offer a rapid development modeller; this allows new ideas to be prototyped to demonstrate how the changes will look. A pilot may use an RPA prototype to test ideas with a small initial audience. The ease of use, low cost and speed of development are all key to testing ideas in an innovation team.
- RPA may be used simply to demonstrate feasibility even if the final solution is different software tool. If this seems odd, it's just a question of using the right

tool for the job, and RPA is not a solution to every problem.
- It's now possible to achieve objectives that would previously have taken excessive manpower.

At each level of the process prioritisation funnel you'll will have a list of processes to assess; the order of the assessment is defined by the information collected at the previous level. This has the effect of narrowing down the list of processes as it passes down from level to level. This means that you can take action at every level in parallel, rather than delaying progress by evaluating every process before you begin. At the higher levels, the criteria provide an overall general view and uses information that can be obtained easily. The information becomes comprehensive for the best candidate processes at each stage, until you reach the bottom of the funnel and pick off the next process you're going to automate.

The information you get from applying these criteria will highlight the right process for you to automate next.

Continuous Delivery

The process prioritisation funnel is a simple, agile approach that works well to prioritise processes for the ongoing delivery of automation using the BUILD-MEASURE-LEARN methodology I talked about in chapter 5.

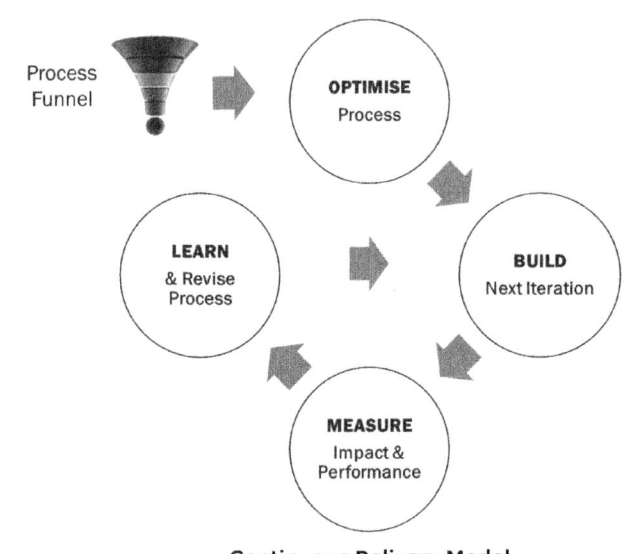

Continuous Delivery Model

Small incremental updates to your automation will help mitigate risk by keeping each change as small as practicable. If you use a pilot to introduce each new release, the risk of errors can be reduced further.

With traditional IT development, new releases of software are infrequent, generally measured in months between each release. This is not the case for RPA; simple tasks can be implemented quickly and the first experiences see benefits delivered rapidly and immediate feedback gives opportunities for improvement.

Automating tasks, rather than end-to-end processes, is only possible through attended RPA so the speed of delivery will be influenced by the selection of software vendor and type of automation. If you think about a typical process that's ideal for RPA, it would generally take 6-8 weeks to achieve the first delivery. Subsequent releases with updates and expansion can then occur more quickly (1-2 weeks) if needed. Processes vary greatly in size, of course, but this is just taking a simple average.

Exercises

> Look at the process prioritisation funnel. Which are the initial processes that you would prioritise at level 1 and level 2?

> Begin thinking about your benefits case: you'll be required to calculate a Return on Investment (ROI). What is your estimated budget (costs)? Over what period do you anticipate payback from RPA? What measurements do you need to calculate the benefits and how will you obtain this information?

Transformation

9. Developing a Target Operating Model

As your experience increases, the way you operate your RPA programme will also evolve and new processes will be established to meet the demands of increasing scale. These stages of evolution are called a maturity model: as your *digital workforce* deployment increases, your operating model will adapt to accommodate these changes in the most efficient way.

During the pioneering phase, you'll adopt an operating model that fits your level of experience, organisational culture and approach. This model will help you to try new things and increase your level of understanding of RPA.

In this chapter I'll introduce three different operating models; they're not unique to RPA but they should give you a foundation for deciding which one best fits your operation. As you scale up, you'll adopt a model that provides the most efficient and effective way of working for your business *at that point in time*.

There are no hard and fast rules when it comes to operating models; the three models described in this chapter have all been used to deliver RPA effectively. If you read the technology press, you may be familiar with the concept of developing a Centre of Excellence; once again this can mean different things depending on the source of the information.

The best way to encourage your stakeholders to buy in to

the organisational and operational changes you'll need to make when you begin to scale up is to explain to them why the new model is right for the future expansion of the operation.

Maturity Model

Throughout this book I've described the stages of your evolving business model. Up until now, it might not have been obvious that the entire structure of this book has been developed around the maturity model:

Getting Started – First Steps
- Proof of Concept
- Cultural Changes
- Suspicion
- Strategy for Staff Concerns
- Developing Skills
- Internal Recruitment
- Narrow Focus
- Celebrate Success
- Low Benefit

Scaling Up – Incubation
- Programme more accepting
- Gaining Traction
- Team Maturing
- Operational Model
- Contract Wide Focus
- Experience
- Process Re-Design
- Company Awareness
- Material Benefits Begin

Transformation – Centre of Excellence
- Embracing Automation
- Top Level Buy-In
- Strategy
- Training
- Standards
- Measurement
- Industrialise
- Full Benefits Realised

Maturity Model

This is a typical maturity model for your automation journey; these are the stages you experience when you start something new. As the concept is introduced, you first take simple steps. As more people become aware, engagement increases and ideas have a chance to incubate and adapt to fit the operation. When everyone is fully engaged, the evolution is complete.

The Maturity Model in the picture above has been tailored to describe our specific RPA circumstances. There is a correlation between operating models and the maturity model and this chapter concludes with a view of the operating models that best support each phase of your evolution.

Getting Started

The first steps you took were a pilot study or proof of concept (POC). The challenge of learning a new technology will undoubtedly come up against cultural issues. You're more than likely to have to deal with people who are suspicious, don't believe in what you're trying to do or have unrealistic expectations of what's possible. Establishing a communications strategy to manage staff concerns has been a topic all of its own. You'll be developing the skills in parallel with implementing automation and to advance more quickly, you'll need to identify people from your existing operations who demonstrate competence in RPA and who can be developed to take on the responsibilities listed in chapter 6.

When your automation programme kicks off, you'll use existing employees to get started; this is the same for any company whether it's large or small. If you have enough money in your budget to bring in a partner or a permanent experienced member of staff, this will help accelerate progress and avoid potential setbacks through inexperience. When you recruit internally, you'll need to match existing staff skills to the six key responsibilities; any gaps will highlight training needs.

Your focus will be narrow during the pilot phase. This helps you learn more about RPA and test ideas safely, as it reduces risk before scaling up. Showcasing your early success stories is an absolute must - it helps others learn about the opportunities RPA provides. Remember that the pilot will only deliver a small amount of benefit relative to what's achievable when you begin to scale up.

Speed is more important than structure during this phase and the operating model adopted is less important.

Scaling Up

Scaling up is what happens when you move beyond the initial pilot processes. You've already worked hard to get your organisation more aware of RPA but you'll still need to introduce the concepts and vocabulary to more people as you start to move into new teams or business areas.

You'll need to change your mindset when you move from the pilot to scaling up. The pioneering stage was very much work-it-out-as-you-go but now you'll need to set up consistent and repeatable processes that can be adopted more widely within your organisation. You'll see there have been two significant changes: first, the team members have improved their skills and capabilities because of the experience they've gained and second, the size of the team will likely begin to increase as well. These changes bring different levels of ability and new levels of specialisation into the team. The team will have to adapt to accommodate these changes so that they continue to work efficiently.

Your pioneers enjoy is the unknown and finding new ways forward, but what you need when you're scaling up a different skill: creating consistent repeatable processes. At this point, you need to keep your pioneers pioneering and find others who are more skilled at establishing repeatable processes.

As your programme progresses beyond the initial process(es) it turns into the incubation phase; this is where you'll be able to develop and test new ideas. At this stage, most people now understand what automation can do and the programme's goals are more likely to be openly accepted.

The operating model now becomes important both for the

team and for the organisation. The focus changes from being very local (pilot) to business-wide, so at this point you'll need to bring more experience into the team. Process redesign is a crucial component, after all, it has been the backbone of this book!

The next step of the programme's development is the creation of a Centre of Excellence (CoE). The CoE's role is to establish standards for identifying and documenting processes; delivering automation; and, measuring progress in real-time. For most organisations, this is the stage at which the full benefits of automation can be realised.

Transformation

Industrialisation and sustainability of your RPA programme will occur as the number of automated processes increases. The cultural challenges are a thing of the past and automation is simply the new way of working, skills are nurtured internally and provide a pipeline of knowledgeable employees engaging to support the increasing resource needs.

The Target Operating Model (TOM) is the blueprint of what your future organisation will look like when you've implemented RPA, and in this stage, you'll be moving closer to achieving the RPA strategy you defined (and continuously refined). Governance and control will be in place for ongoing maintenance and regulatory changes. Although no businesses are completely in this purely operational phase yet, conceptually the operating model will need to change again to reflect the increased emphasis on day-to-day operations and the reduced need for new development.

Arguably no organisation has reached the final phase of transformation, where all possible processes have been automated and the final operating model established. Even early adopters are still working their way through the list of processes with potential for automation. Small businesses will reach this phase more quickly as the size and scale of change is less than in larger organisations.

Operating Model

> It doesn't matter where you start, at some point you'll need to work out where you're going...

Wherever your organisation's starting point for RPA is, there will come a time when you start to think about the pros and cons of developing a Centre of Excellence. You'll find that the lessons learned from early implementations will tell you what works for your organisation specifically. This triggers a move away from a business model which evolves in an uncoordinated way and into a designed - architected - approach for robotic automation.

When you're thinking about business transformation, there are a number of models that you can use to prompt an effective debate about the structure of the future organisation. One of the most common considerations is whether the organisation should develop a centralised or a decentralised approach, or if a combination of both is best:

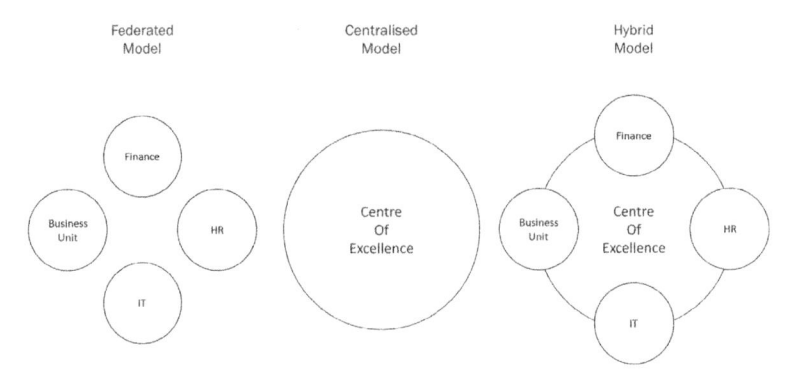

Operating Models

Federated Model

The Federated Model is also known as the Business-Centric, or decentralised approach.

In the federated model, there's no central strategy or direction governing the choice of RPA solution; each business unit or function operates with complete autonomy on decisions. Most businesses that use RPA today started their journey with a small implementation or pilot run in a single business unit.

Many RPA implementations started this way because vendors usually sell directly to business units rather than to the IT department. This results in a functional perspective: a solution that works perfectly for that function but may be unsuitable for other areas of the business. This is where IT involvement can help; they already manage most of the companywide technology services so they're best placed to give you a well-informed view of the solution's suitability that extends beyond a single business area.

This model provides a platform for rapid initial progress especially in the pioneering phase: it's 100% focused on the most critical business needs.

This model has disadvantages as well as advantages. You could end up in with a whole load of different solutions in different business and support areas, particularly if the wider organisation doesn't know what's happening locally. Large multi-national operations have experienced this situation first-hand, for example, when they find a solution chosen by one country can't be used in another. In this scenario they have no choice but to let the situation continue and leverage local skills.

For non-global organisations, the same scenario is more

challenging; available skills are already limited so stretching them across multiple products reduces the opportunities for sharing resources and scaling up.

When I first started exploring RPA, I was surprised to see how often it was implemented without IT engagement. RPA was seen as a quick way of avoiding the lengthy wait times you get with IT projects and IT was rarely sympathetic to engaging on solutions they perceived as another unnecessary layer of technology and not the *proper solution* to the problem.

Increased awareness of RPA is slowly changing perceptions; the views of senior executive teams are changing and the level of engagement is improving. RPA is no longer seen as a *fix,* but a solution that can benefit the organisation both tactically and strategically.

Centralised Model

The IT-centric (centralised) approach is an alternative evolution of RPA which uses the existing software development lifecycle (Waterfall approach) to introduce automation. This model can be far too heavyweight for RPA tools in the pioneering phase and can mean the implementations are slower and more costly. The worst-case scenario is to treat RPA solutions the same way as traditional programming languages; this can result in too much governance and unnecessary levels of design and development.

Every situation is different so the fully centralised model may be the way forward if you've gone for a more technical, development style RPA solution. While I would still advocate using an Agile approach over Waterfall in most situations, a good reason to use this model is when it aligns with the cultural environment within your operation. Fully centralised models *can* be successful but you need to be careful to avoid any unnecessary, and therefore costly, overheads.

At this stage, this is based more on conceptual thinking than on practical experience, but the move to a more centralised model may become the option of choice as organisations reach industrialisation of the *digital workforce.*

Hybrid Model (Centre of Excellence)

It's impossible to say that one of the models I've talked about is best because every organisation differs in size, shape, maturity and culture. When you begin to scale up, many solution providers and systems integrators recommend developing a Centre of Excellence (CoE). What they are referring to is what's known as the Hybrid Model; at its centre is a lightly resourced team with a strong mix of governance, architecture and process skills, surrounded by functional areas who are responsible for their own prioritisation, development and operations capabilities.

RPA introduces a new range of competencies and skills that need to be developed across the organisation. Developing a CoE is an effective way to gather, assess and manage this knowledge and capability, while providing shared guidance to each of the functional areas on operating guidelines and lessons learned from challenges faced along the way.

The hybrid model occupies the middle ground between the federated and centralised models. You may sacrifice a little of the perceived independence from a federated model but you gain the strength of centralised governance, that's optimised and fit for purpose.

If your business is small and you think this section only applies to larger organisations, then you'd be wrong. The key difference is you've most likely started out your RPA journey using the hybrid model and this puts you in a stronger position as you move into this phase. It doesn't matter what size your organisation is, it's still important to define your target operating model clearly.

Benefits and Challenges

As with many new and innovative technologies, RPA is evolving at an ever-faster pace; you need to understand fully how it differs from previous automation solutions to deliver the maximum impact. The CoE's responsibility is to be at the forefront of the advances in RPA technologies to ensure the organisation's policies, procedures and implementations reflect changes while maintaining the flexibility and pace possible from locally-focused delivery teams. Your RPA programme will move from a slow evolution into rapid acceleration with a clear vision and specialist skills delivered by an CoE.

It's beneficial to have a strong link between the business side and IT from day 1; throughout this book I've taken it as read that communications and responsibilities are established clearly from the very beginning. There continues to be a lot of debate about the role of IT and I'll talk about this next. To put it simply, collaboration between the business and IT *will* deliver the best results.

Approach	Benefits	Challenges
FEDERATED • Each business area develops its own robotics delivery function	• In touch and responsive to local needs • No central "overhead" or "oversight"	• Proliferation of technologies • High Variability in skills • Resilience Challenges • Susceptible to resource risk • Higher Costs • Lower Controls
CENTRALISED • A single centralised team of robotic automation expertise	• Resource resilience higher as skills shared across all activities • Allows focus on biggest impact (cost benefit) first • Better utilisation of niche skills (eg. Architecture)	• Lacking Responsiveness for all business areas • Difficult to stay "in touch" with local business area priorities
HYBRID • A core team defining standards, architecture, technology and controls • Closely linked with local teams who focus on specific process automation and ongoing maintenance	• Balances Responsiveness and Resilience • Consistent approach provides cross-company sharing	• Delivery is not in highest benefit order • 1st Level Technical Support is placed in business functions • Version Control is a local responsibility

Operating Model – Benefits and Challenges

Two key lessons from the pioneering phase were:

1. Regardless of whether your starting point is a centralised or decentralised model, the full benefits of RPA can only be achieved through a hybrid approach: local knowledge and flexibility with the benefits of a standardised and resilient set of core capabilities.
2. Collaborative IT/business engagement is critical to success, both sides having open minds.

One size never fits all and, as I highlighted when discussing the business fit and technology fit all the way back in chapter 3, this will help you decide which option (or variation) is right for you. The operating model should be reviewed periodically, as your programme evolves, revising it as your needs change.

The Role of IT

Historically the divide between the business and IT was driven by tales of sluggish IT functions; they are seen as inflexible and out of touch with business needs and/or unable or unwilling to help transform the business.

More recently, a webinar held by Mindfields[46] confirmed the perception of the role of IT: over 80% of participants polled indicated that robotic automation belonged in a business function and 90% believed that a CoE was essential for RPA.

I've worked both inside and outside IT for many years leading software development, business architecture, quality, process improvement, Six Sigma and innovation functions. My view is that the best results are generally achieved when you can put together the right combination of skills and people and that involves finding people both inside and outside IT.

I'm happy to say that the situation is changing and organisations I've met recently have also reached the same conclusion: most people agree that the best results are attained when business and IT combine with a common goal.

First of all, I'll break down the responsibilities that leverage the different IT and business strengths:

Technical responsibilities - defining standards, architecture, training, technology and controls. IT people who understand the need for rapid, responsive, agile and collaborative working are a terrific fit.

---

[46] https://www.linkedin.com/pulse/12-key-takeaways-from-my-webinar-setting-up-centre-sharma-gaicd-/

Functional responsibilities - prioritisation, process automation, development, testing and maintenance. Business people with exceptional technical skills who also understand the need to be responsive to local needs are the best fit here.

Characteristics	Level of IT Involvement	Problems
FEDERATED • Robotic Automation Programmes that are allowed to develop in local functions organically will result in a federated model.	• Little or No IT involvement	• Robotic automation perceived as "non-strategic" • May be missing key skills such as process improvement, standards, version control or architecture • Higher maintenance costs
CENTRALISED • Robotic Automation Programmes that are launched from within the IT function based on software development and change control principles	• Almost Certainly an entirely IT led approach, though a centralised business function is a conceivable variation of this model.	• Governance is too heavyweight for robotic toolset • Less Responsive • Longer development time significantly reduces impact
HYBRID • A core team defining standards, architecture, technology and controls • Closely linked with local teams who focus on specific process automation and ongoing maintenance	• Mixed skills including IT to ensure fit for purpose governance, standards and deep links with change control to respond in advance to changes to underlying systems.	• IT Divide - Robotic automation perceived as "non-strategic" solution and dismissed

Operating Model – The Role of IT

Looking at the different starting points in the table above gives us some insight into how RPA programmes evolve. The federated and centralised models are both insular, involving little cross-functional collaboration. Setting up a CoE is often used as a method of accelerating the pace of RPA delivery and if you're going to succeed, you'll need greater levels of collaboration across functions, business units and IT. The end result will be transformational for your business, but you'll inevitably face a few challenges along the way. In the following sections I'm going to look at some of these challenges so you can understand how a hybrid model CoE can benefit your organisation.

Traditional IT Processes are too Heavyweight for RPA

The word *Traditional* in this context refers to organisations who have a one-size-fits-all approach to technology that often follows a Waterfall process. This means that more time has been spent on documentation than on the actual software development!

RPA tools are a modern class of technology, also known as low-code or business technology. The problem with using traditional IT processes as the starting point for RPA is that business technologies work completely differently to traditional programming languages and can therefore use a simpler governance framework without any extra risks. Too much control will make RPA more expensive and could even derail the business case before you've even started.

I'm a strong supporter of collaborative approaches such as Lean and Agile, and I have no doubt that these provide a more suitable framework for RPA to thrive.

Business Processes lack Technical Governance needed to grow and sustain RPA

IT normally have the greatest understanding of version control and governance; these are part of their standard operating procedures. Anyone who has had to fix code at 2 in the morning will know that good version control and governance procedures are the key to preventing the call in the first place, or resolving the problem quickly if the call does come in.

A low level of control is probably not a big problem to begin with but will become huge when the use of RPA scales up. If you've ever run into the challenges caused by incomprehensible coding of EUC applications or still operating an ancient access database you don't fully understand, you'll want to avoid this outcome by establishing a governance model for RPA that's fit for purpose.

The hybrid CoE is your key to achieving appropriate, fit for purpose governance.

Culture and Acceptance are your greatest challenge

I've met a few IT folks who sit in their ivory towers and tell you RPA is not a strategic solution and applications should be developed *properly*. This might be feasible with infinite time and resource, but in the *real world* we all deal with challenges such as legacy systems, limited time, budget and resource, and so on. RPA *is* a strategic solution; it will accelerate the pace of change and deliver a level of efficiency and responsiveness that's not generally possible with traditional IT approaches.

The culture challenge goes both ways: by the same token, I've experienced initiatives that fail because no one really thought hard about the impact that RPA would have on the organisation. **Employees will be displaced from their current roles**, period. Many vendors want to fluff it up, calling it *natural attrition*, and *redeployment*, but unless your growth plans are significant, that's not going to be enough. Jobs will be lost and people and livelihoods will be affected. If the top-down leadership driving the RPA programme isn't strong, the people and areas most impacted will be able to resist progress and maybe even derail the programme entirely.

The technology is maturing rapidly and provides robust and scalable solutions. Ensure you also have in place the right processes, culture and organisational design.

Unexpected changes to IT systems

The automation software fits across the top of your IT systems and interacts with them in the same way as a system user. Core systems don't change regularly, but they do have occasional new releases and maintenance upgrades. Larger changes may include user training and communicating to everyone who may be impacted well in advance of the change happening. This gives you plenty of time to respond to any questions and to check (and potentially revise) any of your automation scripts in advance.

Small changes can often be challenging as communication is either non-existent or contains insufficient information to identify that the change would impact the automation scripts. Any unexpected changes to your core systems may cause your automation scripts to fail.

The technology used to connect the RPA software to the underlying system is remarkably resilient to change and updates can happen relatively easily, only needing some testing to verify they are still working. Then there is the type of change which is more fundamental, for example, a field moves to another screen; this would need a change to the robot. There are some examples of older software where even the smallest new release requires changes to the automation. These changes are rarely difficult to fix, but advance notification to the operations support team allows them to be implemented to both IT systems and robots at the same time.

Close collaboration between IT and the business is the mechanism by which changes are communicated, giving the opportunity to prepare and synchronise changes to automation at the same time. For larger organisations, an RPA steering group or integration with the existing change control process are the appropriate forums for sharing this information.

Most IT functions have a form of change management in place; IT systems dependencies are identified so all interested parties are notified when there's a change. If you have an existing change management process, including the RPA solutions in that process will provide the feedback and early warning needed to change and test automations.

If you don't have a formal change management process in place, you'll find it beneficial to set up a simple change management mechanism that keeps teams informed about the relationships between applications. The solution doesn't need to be overengineered to facilitate an open dialogue between IT and the business about known system changes.

If the IT systems are maintained by a third party as part of a contractual agreement, you should include a clause in the agreement that requires all users to be notified about planned changes and a test system provided in advance of change. Most third parties don't normally include this clause and you may be unaware that the option exists.

Fine Tuning CoE Responsibilities

Responsibilities	Description	Core Responsibilities	Local Responsibilities
Senior Leader	• Maintains consistency and control of approach	• Standards / SLA Reviews • Process for Robotic Automation • Raise Awareness	• Prioritisation • Categorisation
Business Process Improver	• Optimisation of processes, ready for automation	• Shared Resources for Optimisation: Training, Support, Facilitation	• Initial Assessment and Process Review • Optimisation of processes for robotic automation
Business Architect	• Changing Organisational design to support robotic automation	• Challenge organisational thinking for new robotic operating models	• Implement New Operating Models
Technical Architect	• Provides technology guidance	• Technology Choice, configuration, maintenance • Contract Management	
RPA Developer	• Develop robotic automations	• Testing of new concepts • Shared Resources for Development • Development Standards	• New Robotic Automation Development, Testing and Deployment • Version Control
Operations Support	• Maintenance of existing robotic automations	• Optimising Robot Utilisation across the portfolio	• Maintenance of existing robotic automations, monitoring, re-training, etc.

Operating Model – Responsibilities

In chapter 6 I looked at the six key responsibilities that would be needed in a team looking to develop their first successful RPA pilot. The perspective I took was a narrow view of building your first team. Then, when the programme was being scaled up, the separation of responsibilities gave the opportunity to introduce specialist resources to address bottlenecks as they came up.

Now you understand the Hybrid Model / CoE, the definitions can be further expanded to separate these responsibilities into Core (belonging in the CoE) or Local (belonging in the local business unit). All these roles and responsibilities must be clearly defined and fully understood when you begin developing your CoE:

Senior Leadership

Senior Leadership are responsible for the direction and governance of the CoE, these responsibilities are divided between core (CoE) and local as follows:

Core:

- Establishing operational governance and controls
- Defining standards for compliance and SLA monitoring
- Establishing repeatable processes for RPA deployment
- Raising awareness generally across the entire organisation
- Arranging and chairing the RPA Steering Group (for larger operations)

Local:

- Process selection (Process Prioritisation Funnel levels 2 and 5)
- Educating local stakeholders
- Leading the local business implementation
- Understanding automation options, and categorisation of potential options
- Sharing lessons learned with wider business teams and the Core CoE.

Business Process Improver

The Business Process Improver provides the methodology for selecting and optimising processes prior to automation.

Core:

- Provision of shared resources to help local teams optimise their priority processes
- Workshop facilitation and problem solving
- Delivery of training in business process improvement skills
- Coaching and mentoring for teams first introducing RPA

Local:

- Initial assessment of available processes
- Data gathering to support prioritisation funnel
- The optimisation of processes for automation
- Using local knowledge to accelerate the delivery of improved processes

Business Architect

The core responsibilities of the Business Architect will often be a challenge to traditional corporate thinking and require strong support from the RPA and Executive leadership.

Core:

- Accountable for the overall operating model
- Design and agreement of new operating models to support RPA
- Engaging and educating business units on the operating model
- Monitoring performance of the new model and adjusting as needed

Local:

- Implementation of new operating model locally
- Monitoring impact and providing feedback on performance

Technical/Enterprise Architect

The Technical/Enterprise architecture role is unique as it's the only one that has no local responsibilities assigned; it is a core skill only. This central responsibility provides the technology guidance for the new RPA software and the underlying applications architecture.

Core:

- Validation of the technology choice
- Technical deployment (configuration) of RPA solution
- Performance monitoring, licencing and configuration changes
- Contract management, ensuring all agreements are met
- Regular effectiveness review to ensure requirements are being met

RPA Developer

The choice of technology can vary the degrees by which development is core or local. For example, NICE, where there is a large degree of technical understanding to build the foundation, may locate 80% of the development effort in the CoE. On the other hand, WinAutomation by Softomotive is a simple business solution that can handle 80%-100% of the development locally.

Core:

- Define the development standards for all new deployments of RPA.
- The development and maintenance of reusable components
- Testing of new concepts, horizon scanning and testing of changes to the RPA software
- Provision of shared resources to support local activities to meet fluctuations in critical demand
- Coaching, mentoring and peer reviews for local team members
- Audit and governance to ensure standards are maintained

Local

- Develop and test new automation processes to the standards defined by CoE
- Using local business knowledge and easy access to business resources reducing risk of misunderstandings during development
- Highlight opportunities for reusable automation

Operations Support

Finally, we have the Operations function whose responsibilities are monitoring scheduled tasks, maintaining existing robot automation scripts and correcting any errors in the operational bots.

Operations Support is a responsibility that is added once the number of bots reaches a critical mass that requires 24/7 operations to maintain. Once this level of scale has been achieved, there are benefits to making this a purely centralised function, monitoring, maintaining and optimising the use of robots across the entire portfolio.

Core:

- Monitoring performance of bots
- First level of support for any problems that arise (e.g. Failures)
- Problem escalation if unable to resolve within SLA
- Tracking of known issues requiring long term resolution and identifying solutions
- Planned changes (corporate regulatory change)
- Optimising robot usage across the company

Local:

- Second Level (emergency out of hours) support for problems
- Delivery or Support for CoE of maintenance changes (local regulation)
- Ensure standards are met for bots before promotion from test to live running
- Promotion of bots from test to live running

Exercises

- Where does your organisation fit on the maturity model?

- Which operating model best describes your current situation?

- What immediate changes do you need to make to your operating model?

10. Digital Workforce Evolution

The Automation Delivery Lifecycle (ADLC)

UNDERSTANDING RPA	GETTING STARTED	SCALING UP	TRANSFORMATION
•Raise Awareness	•Training	•Roles and Responsibilities	•Operating Model Design
•Create a Common Vocabulary	•1st Process Selection	•Scale Up Resources	•Implement Centre of Excellence
•Leadership Responsibilities	•Prototype Solution	•Steering Group	•Maintain & Improve
•Understand Business Needs	•Lean Process Optimisation	•Standards and Governance	
•Identify Vendor(s)	•Pilot Study	•Process Funnel	
•Develop Initial Strategy (Vision and Game Plan)	•Development and Testing	•Operations Set up	
•Communicate goal and impact	•Feedback (Build – Measure – Learn)	•Continuous Delivery Approach	
	•Select Vendor		

Automation Delivery Lifecycle

The image above summarises the information covered so far in this book; collectively it forms what is known as an Automation Delivery Lifecycle. It largely follows the Maturity model described in the previous chapter: these are the steps you'll need to follow to grow your *digital workforce* from first principles through to an operational centre of excellence.

The purpose of this book was to give you the knowledge and understanding you need to develop your own *digital workforce*, establishing a high-level plan and locating the skills needed to provide the right level of detail. And the devil is in the detail: getting started with automation is possible for any organisation but when there are complexities of scale, you'll find additional challenges.

Case Study – Approach to Scale

When my business partner and I were first developing our consultancy, we assumed (mistakenly!) that organisations wished to be self-sufficient when developing automation, so we approached the problem to ensure the right skills were developed to overcome the challenges of scaling up.

We found a 50/50 split of views: approximately half our clients were happy to take on the responsibilities of scale themselves but the other half preferred to work with a partner. We now identify this during the insight and pilot phases and that gives us the opportunity to establish partnerships who take on these responsibilities long-term when needed.

In effect, these partners are creating a new type of business process outsourcing by taking on the role of a Robotic Centre of Excellence.

RPA Automation Model

Your primary goal is to introduce a *digital workforce*. The implementation of RPA software and the development of systems and structures such as a centre of excellence to support the implementation are merely the first steps on a larger journey that is made possible by technological advances.

Your RPA programme will give you the foundations that allow you to explore new opportunities and advances in artificial intelligence and become a more innovative company.

So far, this book has consistently focused very specifically on RPA but you may have heard other terms such as Intelligent Automation (IA) or Digital Process Automation (DPA); these are a natural evolution of RPA. The model used throughout this book looks like this:

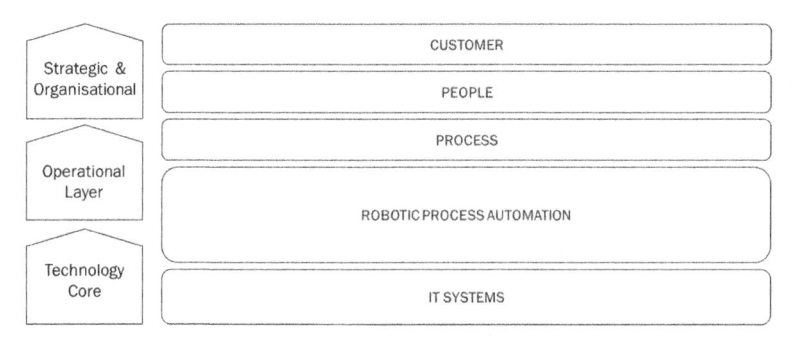

Strategic & Organisational	CUSTOMER
	PEOPLE
Operational Layer	PROCESS
	ROBOTIC PROCESS AUTOMATION
Technology Core	IT SYSTEMS

Automation Model – RPA

At the top of this model are the strategic and organisational goals I introduced in chapter 7 (Lean thinking). These focus on customer demands.

The next layer is operational activities that support the strategy: these are the efficient and optimised processes delivered through RPA.

The foundations of the model are your IT systems: this is the technology layer which provides all the technical functionality.

Intelligent Automation Model

RPA is the solution when the data exists electronically and both data and processes are very structured. If the data isn't electronic, the format unstructured (an email, for example) or the process is unstructured (situational circumstances), RPA alone is not the answer.

The advances in AI are beginning to resolve these shortfalls and give areas that were previously no-go for RPA alone new opportunities to automate.

The combination of RPA and AI is generally referred to as Intelligent Automation.

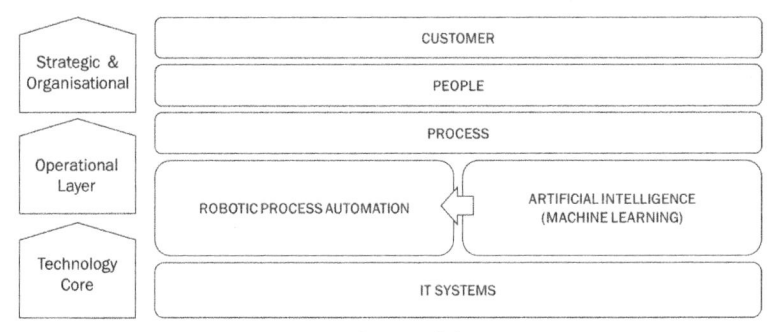

Strategic & Organisational	CUSTOMER
	PEOPLE
Operational Layer	PROCESS
	ROBOTIC PROCESS AUTOMATION ⇐ ARTIFICIAL INTELLIGENCE (MACHINE LEARNING)
Technology Core	IT SYSTEMS

Automation Model - IA

The opportunities for RPA and AI are increasing every day so it's important to keep focused on the specific areas that are most appropriate for your business and not to get lost in the swarm of new providers and technology advances.

The most common example of IA is using machine learning to read handwriting: converting unstructured (handwritten data) into electronic form. How it achieves this is what separates AI from traditional programming techniques.

With traditional programming, every combination of factors has to be known in advance and a programmer writes the code to respond to each of these scenarios. This doesn't work for handwriting recognition, because the programmer would need to reference *everyone's* handwriting and then search for the one that's an exact match when presented with a new document. It would be impossible to get the data in the first place and, even if it were possible, the time it would take for the program to recognise a single character would be too time-consuming to be functional.

Machine learning works differently: the machine is shown different examples of each letter, which enables it to recognise the common elements. Eventually it will be able to recognise letters from handwriting it has never seen before. Machine learning is not programmed in the traditional sense but learns from qualified examples.

So, a machine using AI techniques can learn by example and this now introduces the possibility for it to understand other forms of communication that would be impossible with RPA alone. Take an email message for example. A business may get many emails requesting the same thing every day but each message will be phrased it its own unique style. If RPA could understand the message, it could action the request, but this isn't an option because the message format is inconsistent. At this point, enter AI, which learns what's being requested (classifying the type of message) and extracts the information it needs (structured data) so it can process the request.

Machine learning is advancing rapidly with options for *pre-learned* algorithms capable of interpreting receipts, invoices and standard forms becoming available.

Digital Transformation and Innovation

Machine learning is already being applied to journalism. In the past, compiling sports statistics was done manually by a person and was time-consuming and expensive. Now it can be done automatically by a machine and the customer gets a depth of data and value-add they've never had before. This opens up new opportunities to tailor services specific to a single customer based on their interests and preferences; a degree of detail previously unimaginable.

Machine learning is both producing more data (as in the sports statistics) and consuming more data (such as we see every day in the information we generate from wearables and other Internet connected devices). Every company accumulates an ever-growing amount of data that can also be used to identify new opportunities for innovation and improvement.

The combination of RPA, AI and Data (Analytics) is collectively referred to as Digital Process Automation (DPA):

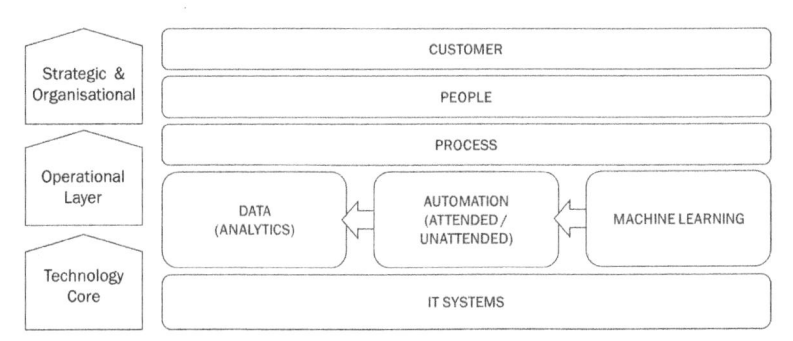

Strategic & Organisational	CUSTOMER			
	PEOPLE			
Operational Layer	PROCESS			
	DATA (ANALYTICS)	AUTOMATION (ATTENDED / UNATTENDED)	MACHINE LEARNING	
Technology Core	IT SYSTEMS			

Automation Model - DPA

Supporters of the DPA model claim that RPA only taps into

a small percentage of the real opportunity and that the full benefits can only be realised through implementing DPA.

Throughout this book, I've advocated using collaborative approaches for your automation teams, such as Agile or the Lean Startup. The Lean Startup is a way to drive innovation and there are many similarities between innovation and automation. The requirements for successfully introducing both innovation and automation are near identical.

A centre of excellence has many of the same elements needed for a successful innovation culture; encouraging collaboration, developing ideas, using short repeating cycles to obtain customer feedback and refine the solution. The reverse is also true: if your organisation already has a successful innovation culture, implementing RPA will experience fewer cultural and organisational obstacles.

RPA produces an increased volume of data as it provides insight into the detailed performance of every automated process you operate; implementing AI also requires high volumes of data so that the computer can learn. This combination gives us more information from which we can now gain unexpected insights and identify new opportunities for improvement.

DPA is the term used to describe the combination of RPA, AI and Data all working together for mutual benefit. RPA provides the automation and generates data that can be analysed to further improve processes and identify new automation opportunities. This data is stored in huge repositories of business intelligence that AI uses to learn. Once it has that knowledge, it is able to understand new situations and automate new tasks through RPA that RPA *alone* was unable to understand. It is a virtuous circle that must have the three essential elements of Data, RPA and AI.

The Next Phase for Automation

The pace of change in RPA has been phenomenal, so it's difficult to make predictions that exceed reality. Having said that, the following topics are high on the agenda for the next evolution of RPA robots:

Self-Healing Automation

Although modern RPA is remarkably stable, it's not infallible. The fragility of RPA is often used as an excuse for not automating regardless of whether or not this is true.

With high volume operations, a process stopping due to unexpected changes to the underlying IT systems can have significant financial impact on business performance. You can, of course, set up rapid response teams to deal with this scenario, but the ideal situation would be for the robot to be able to correct itself and continue processing with minimum delay.

Self-healing robots will be able to identify changes in the underlying IT systems and automatically make the appropriate corrections needed to carry on.

Computer Vision

Computer vision is an existing discipline that uses machine learning to read and understand each screen of information. It uses advances in AI to increase the reliability of reading the screen directly.

Most RPA solutions use internal program object names, called selectors, to reference each field on the screen; even when the IT systems are changed the selector remains the same and so the process can continue unhindered.

Sometimes selectors are unavailable or prone to change; in this situation computer vision is used to read the screen and understand what the information you want looks like. It gives the same outcome as selectors, using a method that's more like screen-scraping, but now applies the advances in AI to make it a more robust option than the fragile approach used historically.

Some vendors are beginning to use computer vision in combination with selectors as their default approach, as it has been identified as being more robust.

The Bot Library

Many development tools have a standard library of useful code that can be incorporated into existing projects simply by pointing and clicking on the item you require.

To prevent the need for many companies developing the same automations, a library of standard automation functions that can be shared will provide an even faster accelerated model for automation.

Major systems providers who have chosen not to develop automation technologies of their own are looking for ways to develop reusable modules with the major RPA providers.

Process Mining and Intelligence

Process mining uses the event data created by IT systems during the normal operation to give insights into how the processes are working and identify the potential for improvement. AI is now being applied to analyse this data and identify opportunities for automation. Several vendors and third parties already focus on these tools to deliver the information back to RPA programmes.

The next generation of process mining is already looking into how this can be taken one step further and, once a process has been identified, it will be automatically be converted into a robot.

There are numerous difficulties with this approach, most notably understanding the real-world context for the process in the first place and evaluating whether it is even needed or could be improved. However, in simplifying and accelerating the first steps on the automation journey this will undoubtedly increase adoption in businesses without the resources to get started.

Although the process may not initially be optimised using this approach, once the process becomes operational, the additional data generated can be further analysed for process improvement opportunities.

Automatic Scaling

Right now, licensing models are still simple, but in future, more complex pay-as-you-go models will allow for automatic scaling up of resources to meet specific peaks in demand or to maintain pre-defined service levels.

Several cloud-based services are offering deeper partnership arrangements where a percentage of income processed is used to calculate the cost of the service. This is a model that can be used to reduce development costs from a business perspective while offering a cash incentive for the service provider to ensure service levels are maintained. In all likelihood this model would be an option from a third-party RPA BPO supplier rather than from a vendor.

Conclusion

If RPA is implemented carefully in a well-planned way, it can be hugely beneficial to any business of any size. The barriers to entry have fallen away and it's clear that a *digital workforce* is the way ahead.

The impact on the human workforce is a genuine concern; I'm generally optimistic, but that doesn't mean there won't be winners and losers. High-cost traditional businesses need to find ways to make immediate savings or they'll struggle to survive against low-cost start-ups. If these companies don't reduce their headcount and number of premises, they risk going out of business completely. Conversely, it's a low-cost enabler to business growth that can quickly and positively impact the bottom line.

As we've seen in this final chapter, RPA is great at dealing with structured information. However, as it is reported that up to 90% of data within an organisation is unstructured, the only way to achieve the full potential is to marry RPA and AI. If you're keen to use AI but haven't started with RPA, then all the lessons in this book apply: start small and build your experience in manageable increments. I would even suggest that getting started with RPA will give you the organisational foundations you need to move into AI in the future.

The best RPA programmes are characterised by strong leadership support, effective business process optimisation skills and a vendor choice that fits the business needs perfectly.

When I first embarked on writing this book, I started with a number of goals. The first was to encourage businesses to sit down and think about their own needs before jumping on the RPA bandwagon and using the first solution that comes along. Developing a *digital workforce* will be inevitable but to maximise your chances of success you *must* identify the solution that has the right cultural fit for your needs to help you avoid the pitfalls of failed RPA projects.

The second goal was to educate, to structure the knowledge that we use regularly in workshops into something that would stand alone in a book format. This was a bigger challenge than I expected in finding the right structure for material to flow naturally. This book will take you from having little or no RPA knowledge to understanding what it can do, to identifying business needs and choosing a vendor, to setting up your pilot team, to delivering your first processes and scaling up. I've found that many businesses lack the courage to take the first step with RPA, so I hope this book gives you the confidence you need to start your own journey.

The future for RPA is bright; the current market leaders (Automation Anywhere, UiPath and Blue Prism) have all consolidated their market positions and are unlikely to be toppled. Having said this, there is room for other vendors to offer unique capabilities that will appeal to different types of organisation. New entrants are now less likely and a few vendors may even find themselves struggling; others may become takeover targets, incorporating their automation capabilities into other software solutions.

In the future, RPA and AI will just be accepted as the way we work. Today that's not the case so it's vital to set up the communication plans and operating models that will help increase understanding and ensure a successful start from which your *digital workforce* will grow.

I hope you found this book informative and helpful and I wish you all every success in your own RPA journey.

Exercise

If you haven't started already, it's time to begin your own RPA journey.

Appendix

Questions Answered

In the introduction, I highlighted four common questions that started me on the journey to writing this book. I've also been recording questions from various RPA workshops and public-speaking events to include in this section:

Where do I begin?

Which is the best solution?

How do I find the right process?

How do I develop a business case?

Can small or medium-sized businesses benefit from RPA?

Can you switch from one product to another?

Do I need a Centre of Excellence?

Can RPA extend the lifespan of your legacy IT systems?

How does RPA deal with unexpected events such as pop-up screens?

Do start-ups use RPA or intelligent solutions?

Can a single vendor provide automation that works on different operating systems and devices?

Why isn't everyone doing RPA?

Can I hire in the skills?

What has been the greatest cultural challenge?

Why do RPA projects go wrong when there's so much information available?

Is there One Ring to rule them all?

Where do I begin?

In the beginning you need to raise awareness of RPA and develop a common vocabulary for all stakeholders and team members. See Chapter 1 for more information.

Historically the places most people start are in their finance and accounting function or back office processing. Back office functions are becoming a more common starting point, so is probably pulling ahead in popularity.

Which is the best solution?

All solutions have their strengths and weaknesses; identifying the best solution means understanding your own business needs. This is covered in Chapter 3; Chapter 4 gives you a comparison of the current top vendors.

How do I find the right process?

Finding the right process is much easier than people think. Many processes are suitable for automation, as they generally have simple characteristics such as taking a lot of time to complete or being very task-oriented using electronic data and systems.

Chapter 5 explains a basic selection approach suitable for the pilot phase; at this point the rigour around the selection process is more generic.

Chapter 8 looks at the process prioritisation funnel: a comprehensive technique for ongoing selection (prioritisation) of processes for automation.

How do I develop a business case?

In Chapter 2 I looked at the key drivers that will provide the foundation of your business case:

- Efficiency
- Cost reduction
- Risk mitigation
- Predictability
- Enabling best practices
- Scalability of processes
- Accountability

Can small or medium-sized businesses benefit from RPA?

Businesses of *any* size or shape can benefit from RPA. Attended or unattended automation and virtual assistants are all within the reach of any business. Even AI algorithms can be used, although the challenge here is not the size of the business but the volume of available data that limits its usefulness.

Most solutions are scalable which means you can start very small and grow.

When a team first gets involved in using automation, they usually love it! You're taking away the mundane tasks, removing the robot from the human. Every business has tasks like this.

Can you switch from one product to another?

There is no migration path or common notation that allows a switch from one product to another, but the question implies a traditional IT perspective which is not necessarily true for RPA.

New technology is traditionally regarded as a long-term investment; you're usually looking at anything between 10 and 20 years lifespan. This perspective of big systems and long-term IT investment influences how we perceive RPA.

The Gartner Pace Layers model[47], which would classify RPA as a System of Differentiation (see below for definition), is a solution that has a high frequency of change, but a medium lifespan. Development times are so rapid in these technologies that it's easier (not easy!) to move to an alternative solution if the software capabilities or business needs change:

Systems of Record: These are established packaged applications or legacy homegrown IT systems that support core transaction processing and manage the organisation's critical master data. The rate of change is low because the processes are well-established, common to most organisations, and are often subject to regulatory requirements.

Systems of Differentiation: These are applications that enable unique company processes or industry-specific capabilities. They have a medium lifecycle (one to three years) but need frequent reconfiguration to accommodate changing business practices or customer requirements.

---
[47] Gartner Says Adopting a Pace-Layered Application Strategy Can Accelerate Innovation. https://www.gartner.com/newsroom/id/1923014

Systems of Innovation: These are new applications that are built on an ad hoc basis to address new business requirements or opportunities. They are typically short lifecycle projects (zero to 12 months) using departmental or outside resources and consumer-grade technologies.

Do I need a Centre of Excellence?

RPA is both a strategic and a tactical solution. Your motivation for RPA and stage of development will dictate whether or not a Centre of Excellence is appropriate for your organisation.

Chapter 9 looked at the topic of maturity models and operating models. Generally speaking, a Centre of Excellence is useful once you take the decision that RPA is a strategic priority or when you begin to scale up.

Can RPA extend the lifespan of your legacy IT systems?

Yes, RPA can provide solutions to extend the functionality available, increasing the lifespan of the legacy systems.

This is an issue for senior leadership: the goal of retiring legacy applications should be separate to RPA delivery. For many organisations the problem is that the cost of technical debt is not that high, so it's less urgent to retire the IT systems. If it does become urgent, then this must be a strategic IT objective.

There's a different concept called the Digital Twin; this is a five-year plan to move from your legacy systems. At first, all your customer records are held on the legacy systems which you then start moving across to the new replacement IT systems at key points such as policy renewal dates. When the five years are up, no data remains on the legacy systems and they can be retired. The digital twin is now fully operational within your organisation. No one has gone through the five-year plan yet but the principle is that all legacy systems are removed within a specific timeframe.

How does RPA deal with unexpected events such as pop-up screens?

This can be a nuisance for RPA and there are different options available depending on the vendor you've chosen. There are a variety of situations where application behaviours change and cause a problem for the bot, these can be broken down into the following 3 levels of complexity:

- Programmatic pop-ups that can be pre-determined can be handled by all vendors as they are within expectations of the process.
- Variable pop-ups that are known about, but where timing is not pre-determined, can typically be handled using trigger-events which only run when the pop-up appears. These popups can be dealt with as they occur, but not all RPA solutions can handle this situation.
- Unexpected behaviours generating pop-ups can be either a minefield of problems or simple to solve. All RPA solutions can lock onto the processing window, so as long as the pop-up doesn't prevent access to the processing window, these situations can be ignored.

The RPA tools that provide the greatest degree of control

over the process flow can handle most situations. However, the basic tools are easier to use because they make assumptions about how they expect the applications to behave, when the application behaves differently it may not be able to handle those circumstances.

Do start-ups use RPA or intelligent solutions?

Start-ups come in all shapes and sizes so this isn't a simple question. Many start-ups begin from the perspective of providing a technical solution to meet customer needs; they are developing their technology ground-up and so the need for RPA doesn't fit with their model.

There are examples of some of the established start-ups beginning to use RPA, but this doesn't appear to be within their core proposition.

Overall, start-ups don't usually need RPA; this makes sense as they don't have the same degree of legacy systems that need to be integrated.

Can a single vendor provide automation that works on different operating systems and devices?

RPA is focused on Microsoft's Windows operating system and all applications that can run within Windows including browser-based applications and virtualised environments.

Why isn't everyone doing RPA?

Many organisations are fearful of change, they're unaware of what RPA can deliver, or they believe the barriers to entry are too high. One of my personal goals with this book is to demonstrate that RPA is useful for every organisation and the barriers to entry are falling.

In consulting, we've found there's a huge gap between organisations that are talking about RPA and those that are implementing it. It *is* a big challenge, but the main challenges are emotions and culture rather than technical capability.

Can I hire in the skills?

The challenge is to find the right people with the right skills, in particular introducing the right mix of skills as opposed to identifying individuals who are expected to do everything; this was covered in Chapter 6. You need to build a team that is capable of covering all the required responsibilities from leadership, process optimisation, development and all the way through to testing, deployment and ongoing maintenance; this all takes time so you'll need to set out a plan to achieve this early in your programme.

Your first call is to find and leverage the great skills within your organisation as they're already there. Hiring staff externally takes more time and costs money.

The market leaders and enterprise builders are starting to dominate sales, so finding these skills externally will become easier, but it won't be easy for a while yet. Even then availability of suitable candidates can vary widely between different countries and regions so taking the opportunity to monitor your local job market will help you find out which skills are more available.

What has been the greatest cultural challenge?

Many expect the greatest cultural challenge to come from the people at the coalface, the staff who deal with customers every day and process the work. They usually embrace the opportunity to get rid of the mundane and repetitive tasks from their roles.

In reality the greatest challenge often comes from team leaders and middle managers. This is because there are fewer of these roles available; they have concerns that their team may be downsized; their scope of influence may be reduced; and their opportunities for advancement become curtailed.

Many change management methodologies refer to the *squeezed middle*, the group of resources below the senior leadership and policy makers, and above the grass roots. They have a great deal of influence and can frustrate your plans if they aren't properly engaged on the programme.

Why do RPA projects go wrong when there's so much information available?

There are many reasons why RPA projects fail, too many to list here. A few of the most common are:

- Trying to automate a process that's too complex and failing to complete the first project successfully
- Trying to automate a process that's too simple and that doesn't demonstrate sufficient benefit
- Assuming it'll be easy and then not engaging the right combination of people and skills
- Being led by the vendor and not thinking about the right fit for the business before starting
- Not working out the total cost of ownership (TCO) and having insufficient funds to scale up
- Disenfranchising your employees before the project has had chance to get going
- Assuming it's going to work for you because you read a successful case study for another business

This book provides a framework which should keep you on the right path. Everyone will experience some form of failure or disappointment along the way; the key is to learn from it and use it to strengthen your programme in the future.

Is there One Ring to rule them all?

No vendor provides absolutely everything. Advances in AI have given most vendors the flexibility to incorporate these algorithms into RPA processes. More examples of multi-vendor installations are also being seen, where different RPA solutions are used to meet certain specific business needs for which they are more suited.

The market valuations of the main RPA vendors are continuing to increase, making it too expensive for mergers or acquisitions to happen. It's likely that we've now reached the peak of expansion; a few smaller vendors will start to struggle, but no single vendor is likely to dominate either.

Glossary

Agile - an approach to software development under which requirements and solutions evolve through the collaborative effort of self-organizing and cross-functional teams and their customers and end users.

Application Programming Interface (API) - a set of clearly defined methods of communication between various computer systems. An API makes it easier to develop a computer program by providing all the building blocks, which are then put together by the programmer.

Artificial Intelligence (AI) - in this book the term is used to collectively describe the different methods and tools which mimic the cognitive functions associated with humans, such as the ability to learn.

Business Process Improvement (BPI) - the act of optimising and improving business processes to increase value. A variety of methodologies and tools exist to assist in this process, lean thinking is one example used in this book.

Business Process Outsourcing (BPO) - the act of outsourcing a task or function to another business, typically abroad where running costs are cheaper.

Centre of Excellence (CoE) - a team, a shared facility or an entity that provides leadership, best practices, research, support and/or training for a focus area.

Chatbot - a computer program which conducts a conversation with a user via text or speech.

Computer Vision - is an element of AI that deals with how computers can understand images. Applied to RPA this typically describes the application of AI techniques to understand and adapt to input forms or changes to the input screens.

Continuous Flow - a term used in lean thinking to describe the efficient movement through a process without error or delay.

End User Computing (EUC) - a set of software tools that can be used to automate tasks without the need for IT knowledge. An Excel macro is an example of a EUC.

Human in the Loop - an approach used to train a computer using AI. When the computer is unable to provide a response it will return the task to a human, from whom it will then learn how to complete the task.

Institute for Robotic Process Automation and AI (IRPA AI) - a recognised industry group who share knowledge and promote the use of RPA and AI.

Intelligent Automation (IA) - the combination of RPA (for process automation) and AI (to interpret unstructured information for RPA to use).

Internet of Things (IOT) - is the Internet extended into the physical world. Its function is to collect data from devices such as wearables, appliances and a vast array of other devices. This can then be transformed into useful information.

Lean Six Sigma (LSS) - a methodology which focuses on improving performance by eliminating waste and reducing variation.

Legacy Systems - an unflattering term to describe old

systems, typically referencing older technologies such as mainframe systems.

Low Code - an approach to developing computer applications without the need for programming; new applications are developed through visual process modelling tools.

Machine Learning (ML) - is a field of computer science that uses statistical techniques to give computer systems the ability to "learn" (progressively improve performance on a specific task) with data, without being explicitly programmed.

Operating Model - a representation (model) of how an organisation delivers value to its customers. The model provides answers to the questions of Why? How? Where? and When?

Payback Period - the amount of time it takes to recoup the costs of implementing a change such as automation.

Robotic Desktop Automation (RDA) - a type of automation that is run alongside a user; also called attended automation.

Robotic Operating Model (ROM) - a representation (model) of how an organisation delivers value to its customers using Robotic Process Automation.

Robotic Process Automation (RPA) - (1) a type of automation that runs independently within a virtual desktop; (2) a generic term that describes the current tools for process automation.

Screen Scraping - an old approach to automation which extracted information from the screens of old mainframe systems for use in other applications.

Selectors - the name given to an internal user interface object that RPA programs link to in order to read and update the information shown on screen.

Service Level Agreement (SLA) - a commitment between a service provider and a client. Particular aspects of the service – quality, availability, responsibilities – are agreed between the service provider and the service user.

Target Operating Model (TOM) - is a future state model for the organisation, the goal state for the organisation.

Technical Debt - the cost associated with running old computer systems or the implied cost of additional rework caused by choosing an easy solution now instead of using a better approach that would take longer.

Test and Learn - an experimental and iterative approach. Similar to the scientific method of hypothesis, experiment, results, but applied to business problems.

Virtual Assistants - a computer program with AI capabilities which conducts a conversation with a user via text or speech.